ZC 24-6670

ANDERSON UNIVERSITY INAS
BV4253 .R68 1924 4229.1
Royden / The friendship of God.

D0421984

Lt. Edmundsbury
M.U. Diocesan U

46

S

THE FRIENDSHIP
OF GOD

By

A. MAUDE ROYDEN

*"Wisdom . . . entering into holy souls, makes
them the friends of God, and prophets."*

G. P. Putnam's Sons
24, Bedford Street, Strand, London, W.C.2

First Published January 1924

SCHOOL OF THEOLOGY LIBRARY
ANDERSON, INDIANA

Made in Great Britain by
THE BOTOLPH PRINTING WORKS
GATE STREET, KINGSWAY, W.C.2

+
BV
4253
.R68
1924

TO
MY FRIEND
EVELYN GUNTER

4229

SCHOOL OF THEOLOGY LIBRARY
ANDERSON, INDIANA

INTRODUCTION

ONE of the sermons in this book—the one called " The Laws of Life "—is the first sermon I ever preached. I preached again in the evening of the same day, but I had no thought but that this would be the end of preaching for me. It never occurred to me that it was an experience likely to be repeated, or that the pulpit was to be to me thenceforward more familiar even than the platform.

And looking back now, it still seems to me that if I had only to preach one sermon it would be that one : for faith in the *trustworthiness of God*—in the fact that he is the same, yesterday, to-day, and for ever—is surely the very foundation of friendship with him. He could not " call us friends " if he were capricious or uncertain, for we should be in fact his slaves. There is no bondage like caprice.

And to many of us God has seemed both inscrutable and capricious. We have not been able to believe that he could " call us friends " : we have remained slaves. The revelation of natural law was needed to make us understand, even dimly, the sublime constancy of spiritual law. We have that revelation now, and it has brought us nearer to our high, amazing destiny—to be the friends of God. This is why I have linked to this series of Friendship two sermons on spirits so—at first sight—far apart as Charles Darwin and Joan of Arc. Both were friends of God in truth, though one perceived "natural" and one "spiritual" law.

A. M. R.

December, 1923

CONTENTS

THE FRIENDSHIP OF GOD

FRIENDSHIP

" Without a friend thou canst not live well."

IT is Whit-Sunday, the day on which the
Church commemorates the outpouring of
the Holy Spirit on Christ's friends. It is
also the first anniversary of our coming
to the Eccleston Guildhouse ; and it seemed
to me, therefore, that the subject of friendship was singularly apt, because the Spirit
of God is the Spirit of love, and this truth
is the heart of the teaching of Jesus Christ.
Little bodies of worshippers like ours here
ought everywhere to be showing the world
what friendship really means. And if there
is one thing that I feel thankful for it is that
some lonely people have made friends here,
and some people who had only a few friends
have made more friends ; and there is a pecu-
liar grace in the friendship we have for one
another when it is associated with service
to some ideal, some high interest, some great
cause. That anyone should have made
friends with anyone else at the Guildhouse
is good for all of us, and specially good for
them. For " without a friend thou canst

not live well," or, in the words of Bacon, " If he have not a friend a man may quit the stage." Indeed the hunger and thirst for friends is felt by almost everyone. There are a great many people in London who are lonely. There are some people who have every opportunity of making friends, and who yet cannot do it ; but I think it is hardly ever because they do not want to. Almost everyone who is human at all desires friends. They may desire nothing else that is good and lovely, but they do desire friendship. " Without a friend thou canst not live well." You cannot even be yourself until you have somebody who loves you and whom you love. You are not half yourself ; you are not half human. You realise that there are in you all sorts of capacities and powers of love which, unanswered, unresponded to, leave you only half alive. People who are lonely suffer in the most acute way, for all their other gifts are more or less wasted if they are never with those whose love for them and understanding of them makes them blossom out like flowers. Without friendship it is true that a man can hardly be human in the deepest sense at all. " Man must be either a god or a beast to dwell alone," says Aristotle ; and Bacon says that that is both true and untrue. A

2

man is not a god who loves to live alone ; but a man must be very near to a beast who does so. Those who desire friends desire something that is a fundamental human need. Love is the very foundation of a man's being. If he has not got it in his life he cannot express himself. Our language, our poetry, our literature is full of phrases about the joy of love. "Fellowship is heaven ; the lack of it hell," is an almost hackneyed saying.

> "Oh, friend, my bosom said,
> Through thee alone the sky is arched
> Through thee the rose is red."

That is not too much to say, is it ? How can you care for the sky or the rose if there is nobody who loves you to care for them with you ? What a tragedy in life to have no one who loves you and understands you ! "The soul of man," says St. Augustine, "was made for God, and is restless until it finds its rest in him." That is only another way of saying the soul of man is made for love and is restless until it finds love.

And yet how baffled sometimes is that hunger for love ! Have you not seen people with great gifts, and with opportunities of making friends, who yet do not make friends ? A boy goes perhaps through his school and college and then enters a business or profession where there are others of his own age ; and yet makes no friends, though he heartily wishes that he could. How does that happen ? What is his difficulty ? It is born of the eternal paradox : " He that seeketh to lose his life shall save it, and he that seeks to save it shall lose it." That is more true of love than of anything else in the world. Remember, all those of you who have no great personal friend and yet deeply desire one, or those of you who have just made a friend and are rejoicing in the friendship, remember that all love is governed by this paradox. If your one desire is to be loved, to be wanted, to be valued, you create around you a barrier over which love cannot reach. The very intensity of your desire for what is in itself a lovely thing seems to repel that loveliness. People may like you, respect you, value you, and yet you will not find that which is the heart of friendship, you will not create that sort of love for which your very soul is thirsting, because you are chiefly thinking, not what you can give, but what you can get. People have over and over again said to me, " I only want to be loved ; I only want to be of use." Is that a small thing to ask ? What on earth could a man want *more* than to be loved ? " I only want to be

4

loved." He that seeketh love shall lose it, because there is some strange quality in that desire for love, that desire to *get* rather than to *give* which isolates him, which makes him lonely. I speak of what I know. I do not think that there is anyone here who desired friends more than I did when I was a girl, or had them less. And I am persuaded that it was because I was more concerned with my desire to be loved, my desire to be wanted, than I was conscious of other people's desire to be loved and to be wanted. And the first thing you have to do (and, indeed, it is the hardest thing of all) is to forget your hunger and thirst for love, and to remember that all the world is hungry. You, perhaps, can give even when you cannot get.

That seems indeed almost impossible to some of us. But we have often to pray " Lord, make that possible to me by thy grace, which by nature seems impossible." For the lonelier you are the more impossible it seems to put aside yourself, and to ask " What can I *give* ? " instead of " What can I *get* ? "

Sometimes one asks a lonely person to make friends with another lonely person, and he refuses because that lonely person is not just the kind of person he wants to make

5   B

friends with. He says he wants to make a friend of somebody to whom he can look up. But if everybody would only make friends with people to whom they could look up, there would not be any friends at all ! And the incapacity for making friends may become a habit. It is a habit that becomes fixed. Break it while you are young. Acquire rather the habit of being more interested in others than in yourself. If you can only get into that frame of mind, you will find as the years go by that you are one of those for whom friendship is assured, because people know instinctively that you are more concerned with them than with yourself ; and this is what makes friends. This is the genius of friendship.

And when you have your friend, what then ? Perhaps you have wanted a friend very badly, and you have suddenly made one, and the thing is so joyful and so absorbing that you feel yourself in the seventh heaven because at last you have found a kindred spirit ; and you become so absorbed in your friend that you have no time for anyone else. If you feel like that, be on your guard. It is a bad sign, for your habit of making friends ought to grow, and an absorbing friendship very often dies because it is exclusive. It should not be so. The fact that you have got a

6

friend ought to make it much easier for you to make other friends. You ought to be able to realise that people who are better than you or worse than you, people who are older or younger, who are richer or poorer, who are wiser or more stupid, have all got capacities for friendship, and it might be possible for you to make friends with them all. I once knew a boy who was able to make friends with his aunts! I think that was the most striking instance of the victory of grace over nature that I have ever noticed; but it shows what is possible. Only remember that if your nephew is willing to forget that you are his aunt, you must also be willing to forget it too. When parents wish their children to be their friends, they must sometimes speak to their children as man to man. And if the child is to forget and ignore the immense disadvantage of your years, you must also a little disregard the prestige of your parenthood. If we can do that in our homes then there is no place where we cannot do it, for there are special difficulties in the friendships of relations. One's family is apt to have such a fixed idea about one. They know so exactly what we are like—and we know so well that we are not like that at all! And the difficulty of getting over this barrier is great. But in the home one has the most crucial experiment

7

ready to hand. A father can make friends
with his own son ; a mother can make
friends with her own daughter. And if you
young people can—not only *love* but *make
friends* of your parents—you are equipped to
be a friend of all the world. For friendship
is often most difficult for those to achieve
who have grown up together and think they
know each other very well.

When you have won your friends you have
to keep them. There are people who are
jealous of their friend's friends, of their
friend's work, sometimes of their friend's own
past, present and future interests. To be
jealous of your friend's friend—that strikes
at the very heart of friendship. To want to
keep a friend to yourself so that no one else
may share at all—there is a vice of which
one may well be ashamed. And yet is there
any vice on earth more common, more
hard to bear or more hard to conquer ?
If God is just, surely he will not punish
jealousy, for jealousy punishes itself ! It
destroys love more than any other quality
in friendship. It is so suffocating, so
stifling, that it destroys love itself at last.
The friendship of the jealous soul is associated
with continual reproaches and bitterness and
anger ; and love cannot flourish in an atmosphere like that, however much the beloved

8

desires it. "He that seeketh to save his life shall lose it." You cannot allow jealousy to enter in without damaging, if not in the end destroying, the relationship between you and your friend.

Above all beware of being jealous of your friend's own reserves. No human being will, or ever can, tell you everything about himself. He would be a shallow person if he would or could. This is a hard saying ; for when a very close and happy friendship is made— when there is equality of age and intelligence and interests and character, and so on, we seem so near to having everything, so near to an absolutely perfect union of spirit, that it seems intolerable to leave even the last barrier standing ; it seems impossible not to disregard the last reserves. But if you do that, you create a sense of violation, for it is not possible to possess the whole of another's soul. Irreverence for the reserves of a friend results in revulsion on the part of the beloved. You have forced your friend to try to give what he or she *cannot* give. There is left a sense of violation.

Do not clamour for spiritual gifts. If they are given under coercion (love can terribly coerce), they are apt to leave behind a sense almost of hatred. To be ready to understand, that is indeed a part of

9

friendship ; but to clamour for the right to understand all—no, no, that is intolerable ; that is a thing that the human soul cannot endure. Those who seek it are, in fact, asking for that which they will not themselves give. Who will so give himself away ? Who does not ask himself at times whether anyone who knew us as we really are could love us ? Those who ask *everything* are asking for that which they will not themselves give. I doubt if there is any human being who has not sometimes a fear at the back of his mind that if he were perfectly understood he could not be greatly loved. That is what makes the friendship of God so supreme a gift. For, indeed, though we know we cannot be absolutely and utterly unreserved with anyone, we often wish we could ! Those exaggerated expressions of unworthiness with which we sometimes approach our friends—those vague assurances that we are not half as good as they think us—are they not a piteous attempt to be frank without being frank ? To be known and yet not known ? We long to be understood, yet we shrink from understanding. We will not tell all. And, indeed, who could ? Try to tell your friend what you are : he does not understand ! Human language is not sufficient to convey all that you wanted your friend to know. And this teaches us, I think, that there must be some final reserves, some sanctuary into which we cannot ask any human being to enter, and which, therefore, in all our friendships with others we must respect.

It is true that we want people to understand us. We want them to know about us, not everything, but a great deal. Love ought not to be blind, for the love which insists that we are something infinitely better than we know we are, really makes us unhappy ; it makes us afraid ; we know it cannot last ; our friend will find us out, and there then arises in us a keen sense of injustice that he should be indignant at finding that we have faults. People insist on believing that their friends are perfect, and when they find out that they are not, their indignation and rage at finding " How many a spot defiles the robe that wraps an earthly saint," makes them feel that they cannot forgive their friends at all. You remember how on one occasion Shelley invited to his home a certain lady whom he believed to be an ideal character, an angel in human form ? Perhaps you will not be surprised also to learn that after a short stay the angel was always referred to by Shelley as " the Brown Demon." Love ought not to be blind. It is not real love that cannot see. To understand one's friend is of all services the greatest, for it gives rest to the soul of our friend to know that although we cannot know him altogether, yet fundamentally we know him, and knowing, love.

We could arrive at a solution of many of the problems of friendship by studying our Lord's relation to his friends. It is one of the adorable qualities of Christ that even among those who were near to him he had friends who were more friendly than other people ; and if we studied his relation to these half-dozen for whom he evidently had a special love, we should arrive at a just conception of what friendship asks of us. To begin with, it rules out at once the difficulty of inequality. Some people think they cannot make friends except among their moral equals or superiors. Christ then would have had no friends ! Yet Christ's friendship with his disciples was a most perfect thing. He trusted them with his life, and trusted them with his word. And at the last he leant on them, desiring their love, and was hurt because they could not respond, as when they slept in the Garden of Gethsemane. Nevertheless, he is with them almost startlingly sincere. He said once to Peter, " You will fail me to-night three times." And a friend of mine once said to me that it seemed strange that Christ should have said that. Ought he not to have assumed that Peter would not fail ? We are taught to-day that we should expect success and we shall find it. And that is so true that one sometimes forgets that it is not the whole truth. Think of what is good in your friend. Think of him as highly as you can. But do not pretend to see *what is not there*.

What is true of human nature ? Why, that it almost always responds to love ; that when it loves it desires to serve ; that when it fails, nine times out of ten it is because of some misunderstanding, or sudden panic ; that such failure does not always mean fundamental wickedness, although on the surface it seems to. That is true of human nature, and that our Lord understood. He expected the best possible, but he did not pretend. And I think that we in our friend-ships would often be much more secure and much more happy if our friends also treated us with fundamental sincerity, not pretending that we are better than we are, not refusing to see us as we are, with all our faults upon us ; but seeing us *as* we are, believing the best possible of us, and still loving us. To be understood, and yet valued and loved— that is peace and joy indeed. Without this, there is always anxiety, fear that when one's friend knows all, affection will die ; dread

that we shall not always be loved. Do you
know that tragic little verse :—

> " Alas, that neither bonds nor bars,
>   Can certify possession.
> Torments me still the fear lest love
>   Died with its last expression."

That kind of fear has haunted most of us who
have loved a human being—the fear that it
cannot last. Who is it that can promise that
it shall last ? Who is it that can swear that
whatever you do he will still love you ? That
person who really understands that you are
human and fallible, and may even fail, and
who, nevertheless, loves you ! To love your
friends truly is to know them capable of
great things, to know them actually possessing
great things ; but it is also to know that they
may fail, and to love them all the same. If
we could love one another so, how gracious
would our friendships be, how secure, how
free from fear, how free also from jealousy
and doubt, how full of that grace which
comes from full assurance ! And if God can
treat us so, knowing us through and through
as we cannot even know ourselves, and yet
loving us and trusting us, and expecting
great things of us, surely we can treat each
other so, who, unlike our Lord, have ourselves continually to be forgiven.

14

THE FRIENDSHIP OF GOD

I TOOK last Sunday a text which was really only half a text. It was from "The Imitation of Christ": "*Without a friend thou canst not live well.*" Those of you who are familiar with that great book know that it goes on like this: "*And if Jesus be not above all thy friend thou wilt be very sad and desolate.*" "Very sad and desolate" because there is not any human friend who perfectly understands you, or always understands you. "The heart knoweth its own bitterness," even as the heart knows its own aspirations, its own ambitions, its own joys, its own shame. Even those human beings who live close together, whose friendship is almost perfect in its harmony, never absolutely know one another. And the very fact that their friendship is so perfect, that they are so exquisitely in accord, makes the slightest jar an agony. With ordinary friends who do not understand you well, you do not suffer so keenly; but in proportion to the nearness and the perfection of your understanding, that failure to understand (which is bound to happen sometimes)

15

is an agony. So that it is true to say, even
of people who have very perfect friendships,
that they are sometimes desolate.

When one reads of the way in which our
Lord treated his friends, one realises the
feeling that prompts the desire for a perfect
understanding. That saying of Rudyard
Kipling's—" Only the Master shall praise us,
and only the Master shall blame "—expresses
a peace that one wins only perhaps after
years of struggling to get the praise and the
just blame of our fellow human beings.
We realise at last that this is impossible ;
that we are asking for what we can never
give, for no one of us always praises and
blames justly. And we desire with Kipling
that only the Master, only God, shall praise
us, and only God shall blame. Let him
blame us. The proudest man does not really
resent blame if he feels it to be just and knows
it to be prompted by love. Perhaps it is not
possible that it should be just unless it is
prompted by love. I do not think it is.
Perfect justice means perfect love.

One of the things that strikes one most in
thinking of our Lord's attitude to his friends
is the extraordinary severity of his rebukes
and the apparently complete absence of
resentment on their part. One is inclined to
think that perhaps the evangelist did not

chronicle the resentment. Yet if you read
the Gospels and see the almost brutal candour
with which the authors set down the record
of the stupidities and mistakes of our Lord's
disciples, you will, I think, believe with me
that if there had been resentment it would at
least sometimes have been recorded. And
there is no hint of it. Our Lord says to one
of the dearest of his friends, " Get thee behind
me, Satan ; thou art an offence unto me :
for thou savourest not the things that be of
God, but those that be of men." To James,
to Philip, to Nathaniel, and even to John the
beloved disciple, he addresses words of criticism and blame, sometimes almost terrible in
their severity ; yet there is a complete absence
of resentment. Surely this came from the
fact that the disciples realised that our Lord
loved them intensely ; that he knew their
goodness, and, indeed, was much more interested in it than in their badness. When
they were bad he rebuked them, but it was
not their badness that occupied a prominent
place in his mind ; it was their goodness. He
saw the glorious possibilities that there were
in that little band of disciples. They were
to be the light of the world. They entered
into his most sacred experiences. He loved
and trusted them. Surely that is why they
never resented his anger against them,

17

SCHOOL OF THEOLOGY LIBRARY
ANDERSON, INDIANA

4229

although they must have been wounded
by it.

Such sincerity kills sentimentality. We
easily become sentimental because we are so
often insincere. Even a very noble interpretation of Christ is sometimes spoiled by
sentimentality. Read this passage, for example :*

" They [the disciples] spoke of the things they had
heard the people of Tyre and Sidon say, and of what
men were saying of Jesus.

"' One man said he was John the Baptizer, new
risen from the dead,' said a disciple, while another
said :

"' 1 heard a woman say he was Elijah.'

"' No, it was Jeremiah,' said a third.

"' They all said he was one of the old prophets
who had risen again to help us,' said another.

" Suddenly Jesus turned to them and said :

"' And who do you yourselves say I am ? '

" The disciples, taken aback, looked at one another,
but did not answer. Peter kept quiet for a moment
pondering, and then his mind seemed to make a jump,
and he cried out, his eyes bright with love and enthusiasm :

"' I say you are the Messiah.'

" Jesus looked at him, and there was a great
affection in his eyes, but his voice was sad when he
spoke.

"' Do you know what it means to be a Messiah,
Peter ? ' he asked. Peter shook his head. Jesus
went on, speaking as a man speaks of things long
thought over . . .''

* From an Unknown Disciple.

According to St. Matthew, when St. Peter recognised who our Lord was, our Lord cried out with joy: " Blessed art thou, Simon Barjona : for flesh and blood hath not revealed it unto thee, but my Father which is in heaven." In the account given by the " Unknown Disciple," our Lord does not rejoice. Peter has said a very true thing, but Peter is not at all a perfect person, and so he looks at him with great affection, but " his voice is sad when he speaks." I do not think it was sad. I do not believe that Jesus always bore in mind when you did something splendid that there were other things you had done which were not splendid. I think he forgot them in his joy. I believe he rejoiced in the good thing you had done without preserving a perpetual attitude of pain because of the bad things you had done also. Only very exasperating human friends are perpetually " pained " at one's past and future misdeeds. The Jesus of the Gospels was not like that. He denounced Peter with all the vigour with which he had praised him, but Peter was able to endure the rebuke because he had still in his heart the glory of the praise. That we should be a friend of one who, for our sakes, is indignant when we sink beneath ourselves, but not a whit the less joyful when we rise above ourselves, should make us almost

19

immune from the desolation of spirit that comes when our earthly friends do not understand us. There is no one here who has not felt that desolation of not being understood. It is not by any means always due to the fact that people do not think well enough of us. It is sometimes the knowledge that they think far too well that leaves us with a sense of loneliness. To be in the relation of friendship with one who knows all our goodness and all our badness, and, knowing it with a clearness of vision that we can never attain ourselves, yet loves us, gives us a sense of deep security and peace. After all, there is no joy on earth like that joy ; nor should we resent the pain that comes of being rebuked, because of the happiness of being wholly understood.

For all of us such friendship is possible. It is the friendship of God. I speak of something which to many of you here seems to put too human an interpretation on the idea of God. God, you think, is something more than personality. He is not personal, he is " immortal, invisible, inaccessible, hid from our eyes." He is the principle of creation ; he is the principle behind the universe. To imagine that you can have with him the intimate relationship of a friend is, to some of you, to attribute to him the limitations of human personality, and the conditioned char-

20

acter which we are accustomed to associate with personality. And unless God is in some sense personal, to talk of friendship with him in any real sense is absurd. There is no such relationship as you and I mean by friendship, certainly nothing at all like that which our Lord had with his disciples, between the absolute principle behind the universe, and you and me. Such a relationship is impossible; and, in fact, if you pursue the thought a little further, I believe you will ultimately come to the conclusion that no relationship at all is possible between ourselves and a wholly impersonal God. Even in that lovely Christian hymn we sang just now, how many negatives there are about God—*not* mortal, *not* visible, *not* accessible, *not* resting, *not* hasting, and so on—because when we think of God as Absolute Being, we cannot describe him in anything but negatives. He is *not* limited, he is *not* conditioned by any of the things we know, he is *not* visible, he is *not* changing; and in the end you will realise, I think, by such a process as that, that he is *not* anything you can think about at all, and you become in the highest and purest sense of the word an atheist. You are reduced to the thought of absolute negation; and no one can think a negation. God is none of the things we know, and so he passes beyond our thought altogether, although

21 C

we may still affirm that something is there, that there is a vast creative principle, an absolute God ; but since we cannot think of him in any terms whatever, we are not able to think of him at all. The purest form of such a religion is, of course, Buddhism. This is not true of popular Buddhism as practised and believed by the ordinary average Buddhist, who like the ordinary average Christian, is probably no theologian. But in fact the denial to God of all attributes which the human mind can realise, ends in atheism.

Now it is not possible for there to be anything in creation which does not come from the mind of God. (I have to use such human terms as " the mind of God " because, as Dr. Stanley Mellor says, when we speak of things ineffable we stammer.) Nothing is here, then, which is not in the mind of God. If you and I are persons, then personality must exist, must be included, in the Godhead. To imagine otherwise is to imagine an impossibility. There cannot be anything which has not come forth from God, and that which comes forth from him must be of his own nature. If you and I are personalities God must include personality, and if we had always spoken of him and thought of him as including personality, and not as being " a person," probably that truth would never

22

have been lost sight of. Christianity has done its best to keep us in mind of that great principle in the doctrine of the Holy Trinity, and this is Trinity Sunday. What does the Trinity mean ? It sounds an academic question, and I could give you some very academic replies. But the doctrine of the Trinity is no academic or purely intellectual puzzle, no invention of hair-splitting theologians ; it is a doctrine which you will find in the greatest religions of the world. Surely that is because it is not a figment of the intellect but an eternal truth. When humanity arrives at the point of developing a great spiritual religion, it produces a doctrine like the doctrine of the Trinity. What is at the heart of it ? God is not " a Person," and whoever says so is heretical. God is absolute ; he is infinite ; he is something infinitely greater than a person, although he includes personality. The way in which this can be most easily expressed is to say that he is one God, but three Persons ; a Trinity like Beauty, Truth, and Goodness, like body, soul, and spirit, like many other fundamental things. Three is a mystic number expressing the infinite and immeasurable. Deity is three Persons in one God. In the Godhead, therefore, there is included that wonderful thing which we call " personality," and it is

23

included in a sense far beyond our imagination. Personality is not less in the Godhead than in us. It is, there, more wonderful, more complex, than we, with our limited little minds, can possibly imagine. All that we can do is to put it in this mystical form and say that God is Three in One, and One in Three, and that his being does indeed include that which is the highest thing we know, although we know it in so imperfect a form—personality.

In our greatest moments we can sometimes, not indeed comprehend, but apprehend the Eternal and the Absolute. Our souls perceive the absolute and eternal God. "No man hath seen God at any time," but all of us have the instinct of perceiving God sometimes, in perfect love, in perfect beauty. Suddenly there is flashed upon us the sense that there is "a depth beyond the depth and a height beyond the height, our hearing is not hearing, and our seeing is not sight." For a moment we have been with the absolute, the eternal God. These are our highest moments. For the rest—we live in time and space.

There are people who in their anxiety to escape from the irreverence and stupidity of thinking of God as a human being put aside the very idea of friendship with God, and deny themselves the sense of his intimate

24

affection for each of us, thinking, "How is it possible that the absolute God should know or care about anything so small as myself?" Have you not all of you felt that sometimes? You have griefs and difficulties which mean everything to you, and perhaps tradition and custom teach you to bring those problems to God; but then there sweeps over you the sense of God's infinite power, and your own microscopically small concerns, and you feel that it is a folly to suppose that your little human affairs can be of any interest to God.

When we try in that way to escape from too human an idea of God, we are really falling into it more deeply than ever. We not only think of God as a man, but as that very odious kind of person, a busy man, a man who is too great and important to see anyone but the heads of departments! He has the universe to look after; how can he look after you and me? He is such a busy person! But is it not the most elementary form of anthropomorphism to think of God in terms of size? If God is absolute and unconditional, the fact that you and your affairs are small, and the universe large has no meaning to him. All things are equally dear and equally present in his mind, and to think otherwise is to attribute to God, not only personality, which you are trying to

25

escape from, but the narrow limitations of human personality. I believe intensely in that personality which God includes, and my religion is the worship of a personal God. The moments that I perceive God as absolute are few indeed compared with those when I think of him as a Friend. But if I were to think of him as a Friend who was sometimes too busy for things so infinitesimally small as myself, I should be thinking of him, not only as a human, but as a most deplorable type of human. Even we who live in time and space rebel against the limitations which make it impossible for us to love all the world, and to make a friend of every person whose friendship we desire. To think of God as though he were so conditioned were anthropomorphism indeed. Even we ourselves hope to transcend such limitations some day.

So I beseech of you to think whether it is not possible that in the mind of God greatness and smallness, as we think of them, do not exist, just because, although he includes personality, he is absolute and unconditioned, and time and space to him are nothing. We are small indeed compared with the great world. And the world, how small in the vast universe! What ranks and ranks of existences there are, so great that we cannot see them, so small that we cannot think them! At what point does the infinite God begin to think that things are too big, or too small to be noticed? How big must you be to catch his eye? There is no size in the mind of God, and when you approach God as friend be sure that your affairs are as dear to him as the sustaining of the universe. " Oh, taste and see how gracious the Lord is."

So gracious is he that some have even claimed that they were God's favourites— that God has singled them out for special favour. That idea is repulsive to us; but think what it means. It means that when you take God for your friend you become conscious of a care so exquisite, an understanding so real, that if you are not a very great person you easily fall into the mistake of thinking that God is taking special care of you. It is a childish mistake. It is the mistake of egotism which is the characteristic of a child. But you see how it arises. Look at the experience of the saints, and you will find that they experienced a sense of tenderness and care and understanding; they walked and talked with God as Friend, so that it was almost pardonable that they should think of themselves as more the friends of God than other people. Such a friendship brings such peace that those who

27

know it, even in the least way, desire beyond anything to proclaim it to the world. For the friends of God know his peace which passeth understanding. They are lifted above jealousy, resentment, and anxiety. They suffer—God forbid that any human being should *not* suffer—when human friends have failed them or they have failed their friends, but their suffering is not to the death of the soul, and in the sanctuary of their being is peace.

SPIRITUAL SIGHT

" Then came Jesus, the doors being shut, and stood in the midst, and said, Peace be unto you. Then saith he to Thomas, Reach hither thy finger, and behold my hands; and reach hither thy hand and thrust it into my side; and be not faithless, but believing. And Thomas answered and said unto him, My Lord and my God. Jesus saith unto him, Thomas, because thou hast seen me, thou hast believed; blessed are they that have not seen, and yet have believed."
—John xx, 26-29.

MY text to-night is the above passage describing our Lord coming into the upper room where the disciples were gathered together, when, for the first time, St. Thomas was present. You remember St. Thomas had said he would not believe that our Lord was risen unless he had ocular witness.

I often think our country and the world in general would be in a healthier state if we had tried harder to discover what were the virtues which our Lord specially loved. The fact that he set a great value on certain virtues ought to make us ask ourselves whether there is not some unappreciated moral value in them. It has been noticed again and again

29

that our Lord was much more gentle to the sins of the flesh than the average respectable Christian is, and much more severe to the sins of the spirit; and that Christendom has, generally speaking, turned that judgment upside down. And here the great emphasis that he lays on a certain quality which he did not find in St. Thomas, but which on several other occasions he did find in others, and rejoiced over, should make us ask ourselves whether there is not some unappreciated moral value in that particular quality. "Because thou hast seen me, thou hast believed; blessed are they that have not seen, and yet have believed."

You will remember our Lord's joy when he found that St. Peter recognised who he was; he did not rebuke the other disciples, but he rejoiced at the spiritual insight of St. Peter. "Thou art the Christ," says St. Peter; and our Lord says, "Blessed art thou, Simon Barjona: *for flesh and blood hath not revealed it unto thee, but my Father which is in Heaven.*" You see the reason why he attached so much importance to St. Peter's confession; it was because flesh and blood had not revealed it to him, but God. Again, he speaks with great joy about faith. "I have not found so great faith, no, not in Israel." You find there a certain quality of

30

joy which makes one realise how much our Lord valued that particular gift. It is not the virtue of patient and careful study of the evidence : it is the virtue of perceiving truth. Perhaps, at first sight, it may seem that here our Lord is quite out of touch with the modern scientific spirit. We admire those people who are slow to believe, who will not allow themselves to be carried away by the desire to believe, but who patiently, laboriously and dispassionately consider the evidence. St. Thomas seems at first sight to be the kind of person whom the twentieth century scientist would admire and commend.

I believe that our Lord had the most scientific spirit of any person that ever lived, and I believe that his love of the quality of insight is love of that quality which to-day, and, indeed, more than ever to-day, makes the supreme scientist. It is the quality which differentiates the student from the genius, the writer from the poet, the workman from the craftsman, the toiler from the creator ; it is that quality of *perceiving truth* even in the face of that which appears to be conflicting evidence. There are students of science who laboriously collect the facts, students, who, like St. Thomas, believe when they have seen. But rare is that quality which perceives, in spite of

evidence dislocated and disjointed, the underlying truth ; and that is the quality which
makes a Darwin and an Isaac Newton, which
makes the supreme genius in science as well
as in art. The discovery of truth is higher
and greater than the discovery of facts.
When our Lord rejoiced over St. Peter's
confession and declaration of his Messiahship,
and when he spoke rather sadly to St. Thomas,
saying, " Because thou hast seen thou hast
believed ; blessed are they that have not
seen and yet have believed," he was not
praising the idle superstition of believing what
is false, he was praising the quality of perceiving what is true. After all, unless we have
that quality we shall have nothing. We
shall never know *all* the facts about anything ;
yet every one of us must in his measure and
degree try to see the truth. It is that quality
of insight which we hail in the truly great.

Our Lord was not harsh to St. Thomas.
On the contrary, with that exquisite tenderness which always went nine-tenths of the way
to meet those who would believe if they could,
he gave him the evidence for which he asked.
He did not say, " If you cannot believe without seeing you must go without believing."
He knew that St. Thomas wanted to believe
and he knew that although his spiritual
insight was not yet very great, yet his love

32

was great. I do not believe there were any of the disciples who loved our Lord more than St. Thomas did. Therefore when he said that he could not believe without this material evidence, our Lord gave it to him. " Reach hither thy finger, and behold my hands ; and reach hither thy hand and thrust it into my side." Here are the material things that you want. Now believe ; but, nevertheless, realise that if you had perceived that it was not possible for the Eternal Spirit to be held in corruption, that would have been greater still. Again and again one notices our Lord's gentleness to those who are trying to see what is the truth and who sometimes believe for such strange reasons. It seems a curious reason for believing in the resurrection —that one should see the wound prints in the body. Ought they not to have known that Christ was to suffer and to conquer ? " O fools, and slow of heart to believe all that the prophets have spoken."

In the narratives of our Lord's appearances to his disciples after the resurrection, one realises how often they failed to recognise him at first. It is evident that there was some change in him, for hardly ever did they recognise him at first sight. Then he said or did something that was characteristic of himself, and they said, " It is the Lord."

33

When he came to them after they had been toiling on the sea all night, and they were hungry, he gave them food, and they said, " It is the Lord," because it was so like him. It was the mark of his spirit that he always cared for those who were hungry and tired, and not only had the love, but the power to do it. When our Lord met the disciples on the road to Emmaus, he enlightened their understanding, and then they said, " It is the Lord." " Did not our hearts burn within us while he talked with us by the way ? " He enlightened their minds and that was characteristic of his spirit. So they perceived that it was he. It was that kind of perception that our Lord welcomed.

This quality which he prized so much can be achieved by all of us. We cannot all achieve intellectual genius, but we can achieve this spiritual sight. It is one which every Christian may possess. You will have noticed that very simple, uneducated people sometimes have it. They are always right. They always know good from evil. They are always wise. They are not deceived. They have that strange perception of goodness which makes the real saint the hardest person in the world to deceive. Yet sometimes they are not at all intellectually clever ; and one is inclined to say of them, " It is easy for them

34

because they were born good ! " It is the
idlest excuse, the most senseless way of
treating spiritual genius that it is possible to
imagine. We do not strive to be as good as
these, and so we say " It is easy for them, for
they have been born good ! It is so difficult
for me." When I see a saintly life discounted,
not indeed admired less, but discounted as
an inspiration to us, because people say
" he was born good," so that something
of the inspiration that such a life should
be to every Christian person is wasted, I feel
very sure that people are not born so good
that they do not need to struggle ; and when
a man achieves such goodness, the thing that
ought to rejoice us about his goodness is
that he is an instance of what other human
beings may become.

How shall we achieve this spiritual quality
of knowing good whenever we meet it ?
Despise no one : do not even despise yourself.
Do not say, " I was not born good." " What
God hath cleansed, that call not thou common
or unclean." Since you are a child of God
do not despise yourself. Do not set yourself
down as a person too commonplace to become
one of the saints of God. Every human life
is holy. Do not hate your body. Do not
mortify your intelligence. Do not despise
your emotions. To do any of those things

35

is to call what God has cleansed, common and unclean. It is God who made your bodies. There are people who think they can get nearer to God by ill-treating their bodies. They are heroic, but they are mistaken. Those Christians who think they please God by stunting their intelligence (as though it had not been given to them by God) are mistaken. Perhaps even more deplorable are those people who despise their emotions, who think that religion should be a kind of hard logical intellectualism without the breath of inspiration and love. It is human to rejoice and to mourn and to love, and to hate that which is evil. To despise anything that is truly human hampers your spiritual progress. All your being was given by God, and all of it, body, soul and spirit, is noble. What you have to do is to create such a unity in yourself that you are able to reflect God who is himself unity.

Here again modern psychology helps us. If we repress anything that is in us, any bodily impulse, any emotional instinct, any intellectual power, we are setting up discord in our being. There is war in our members, to use St. Paul's words. There is war in us so long as we try to suppress some power, some emotion. But the greatest intelligence must have peace before it can work at its best. If the cleverest man in the world neglects his body, and gets indigestion, his brain will not work half as well. In the same way, the person who is wanting to see spiritual things and suppresses impulses and instincts, and despises his body or his mind, is setting up in himself that kind of discordance that prevents his spirit from seeing clearly. The opposite of that suppression is not licence, for licence allows one part of your being to dominate the rest. To give rein to your body is to atrophy your spirit and mind. To give your intelligence play is not to make it master of your whole being. To give your emotions play does not mean that you are to be dominated by your emotions. All these are to be trained and disciplined ; not destroyed, but directed. It is in that way you achieve unity ; and let no one dream they can achieve it by letting go the reins and giving way to indulgence. You must not despise these things ; you must use them ; and you will soon find how essential to use is control and discipline. For God is not discord ; God is Unity and Truth. Therefore, we cannot apprehend him, still less reflect him and show him to the world while our being is full of discord. We may have noble instincts and splendid aspirations, but if there is discord in our hearts we shall lack spiritual perception

37 D

and the power to see God. It is not by repression that we attain it. It is by learning to reverence and to use all the powers that are ours, so that there is created in us that spirit of unity and harmony which in itself is a reflection of the Spirit of God, who is all unity and harmony and power. Here, as I have said, modern science can often help us, teaching us that in every aspect of life these three parts of our being—body, soul and spirit—must have their place. A brainless art, a heartless sensuality, an ascetic or a stupid religion—all these things are discordant; they have in them that war which prevents us from seeing God. We are made in the image of God. We know that because we can see God. We can sometimes apprehend him. If we were absolutely without God in ourselves we could not reach God in any way. It is because the divine spirit is in us that we can perceive the divine spirit without. But if there is discord in our being it prevents us from reflecting God. It is like the sea tossing in the wind, which cannot reflect the stars. The star is reflected in a little pool when it is still, but it cannot be reflected in the whole ocean when the ocean is not at rest. The heart of man can only achieve that unity which enables it to see God, and to apprehend spiritual truth, when it is itself at one. I think that is why at the end of his life on earth our Lord prayed again and again, with such insistence, "that they all may be one, as thou, Father, art in me, and I in thee." Only when we are at one with ourselves can we see God, and only when all Mankind is at one will Humanity itself perfectly see God.

Now in all history the spiritual hunger of humanity has been a great fact ; and it was one of the faults of the science of two or three generations ago that in its reaction from the false spirituality of a misunderstood Christianity it ignored that spiritual hunger. Scientists of to-day have revolutionised our knowledge of the human mind by facing the fact of humanity's spiritual hunger and thirst. It is an obstinate fact in human nature that it desires spiritual things as it desires physical things ; and to have a science which deals only with one, and not with the other, is simply stupid. That spiritual hunger and thirst cannot be repressed or stifled or ignored without atrophying and dislocating your being. This is a fact, and it has taught humanity that there is such a thing as a perception of God. Long before science taught us the unity of existence, the spirit of man had perceived the unity of God ; and even in the most polytheistic religions, in places like

Central Africa and Australia, behind the innumerable and sometimes base gods which people worship, there is the worship of the great Spirit, the great Father. The religion of such people is often so debased and superstitious that one almost hesitates to call it a religion; yet you may always discover behind it a dim sense of some great Spirit who is not even given a name. At the other end of civilisation, H. G. Wells finds behind the warring world and the struggling God that One "behind the veil" Who unifies all things. In the same way Humanity has learned the existence of God—how? Because, in the words of Pascal, "Thou couldst not have sought me if thou hadst not already found me." We could not seek for God if, in a very real sense, we had not already found him; and if there are people here who are seeking for someone who will indeed convince them that there is a God, and he is love, I say to them especially to-night, "Thou couldst not have sought him if thou hadst not already found him."

If you hunger in your body, does it not prove that there is such a thing as eating? If you hunger in your soul, does it not prove that there is a God? How could you desire him if he was not there? How could you seek for him? It is his power within you which will not let you rest. It is God already in your heart that urges you on to the search of God. By what devious paths, by what human or divine help you will find him, I do not know. But I beg you to consider whether it is not true that the fact that you have the desire in your heart proves there is a God to answer it. To repress that desire, to ignore it, is as unscientific as to repress your emotions, to stunt your mind, or to starve your body. The desire of the spirit is as real as any of these things; and in the light of modern science you know you must not rest from that quest, or ignore it.

Perhaps it is easier for the less gifted natures to find that peace and unity than for the great ones. In that sense, perhaps, there are some to whom goodness is, I will not say "easy," but easier. It is easier to regiment a little army than a great army. It is easier to set in order a little household than the affairs of a great world. It is easier for those who have smaller gifts to discipline them and unite them in the service of God. It may be very hard for those whose intelligence is very keen, or whose bodies are very hard to control, or whose emotions are very tempestuous. It may be harder for them; but when it is achieved it is a greater thing.

41

The pool may reflect the starry heavens, but a great lake will reflect it more majestically. Those great people with great powers who are thus able to achieve the unity which sees God are, after all and in the end, those who most uplift humanity. If there are people here who by the very keenness of their intelligence, or the strength of their passions, or any other God-given gift, find it very hard indeed to see God, let them take this for comfort : that when they see him, when they achieve that spiritual perception which sees the truth and knows it, they will proclaim it to the world with a power that is in proportion to the travail with which they reached it.

A MODERN PROPHET:
CHARLES DARWIN

" Whosoever speaketh a word against the Son of Man, it shall be forgiven him: but whosoever speaketh against the Holy Ghost, it shall not be forgiven him, neither in this world, neither in the world to come."—Matthew xii, 32.

THE man I am going to speak about this morning, Charles Darwin, is one of about a dozen men whose lives have marked an epoch in the history of the world. It is a tremendous thing to say about any human being that, because they lived, the world itself is changed. But it is certainly true of Darwin, and it is so true that, when one tries to realise what it was that he did, one finds a difficulty in doing so. His success was so overwhelming, and the change be made in our habits of thought so fundamental, that it is difficult for the modern man or woman to understand what all the trouble was about —to realise the point of view of people who really believed that the writing of a book like " The Origin of Species," or " The Descent of Man," made belief in God impossible.

43

The state of mind of people whose whole faith in God was shaken by the formulation of the theory which we call evolution is so remote from us that when one tries to put into a sentence what it was that troubled them, it is exceedingly difficult. Probably a great many of us do not even know what it was that upset people so much, but, briefly, I think it was this.

People, before the coming of Darwin—at any rate, theologians and many orthodox religious people—believed that their faith lived or died, stood or fell, by a literal interpretation of the first chapter of Genesis. I lay some emphasis on the first chapter, because, had they taken the trouble to look, they would have found that the second chapter of Genesis gives an entirely different account of creation from that in the first, and how any human being is able to believe at the same time two entirely different accounts of the same event I do not understand; but it seems that unless you were prepared to believe that when it came, for instance, to the creation of fishes, God said suddenly: "Let there be fish," and immediately the ocean teemed with just such fish as we know; and on the following day God said: "Let there be birds," and immediately there were birds—unless you were prepared to believe that as

44

literal history you could not believe in God
at all.

Darwin showed, and showed with a clearness that converted the world practically in
a generation, that whoever created the world
and the things that are in it, they did not
spring into being on Monday, Tuesday and
Wednesday in a certain week in the year
4004 B.C. ; but, on the contrary, developed
with slowness so extreme that for a long time
there was a grave quarrel between the
geologists, who said the world could not
possibly be more than twenty millions of
years old and the evolutionists, who de-
manded a much longer period than that in
which to allow for this slow process of evolution. And in proclaiming this, Darwin appeared to the religious to be destroying their
faith in God. I know people often feel that
the moment one begins to speak of the first
chapter of the Book of Genesis as not being
a literal, historical or scientific account, one
is " explaining it away " altogether. It would
be as reasonable to take, shall I say, two or
three lines from Wordsworth's " Ode on the
Intimation of Immortality," and three or four
thousand years hence to say of them—" This
inspired writer affirmed that ' not in utter
nakedness, but trailing clouds of glory do we
come from God, who is our home,' and that

everyone who affirms that babies are born in a state of nakedness is flying in the face of this inspired writing!"

If you read the first chapter of the Book of Genesis you will see that it is a poem. You will notice that the end of each passage is marked by a refrain, " The evening and the morning were the second day." "And God saw that it was good." " And the evening and the morning were the third day." And so on. It is a poem, and it is as nobly, magnificently true as any of the great poems in all human, religious, or poetic literature.

When, however, Darwin said that "creation" really took incalculable ages, and that all species started from one, not only the theologians, but even the " orthodox " scientists, fell upon him and said he was destroying almost everything they had believed.

The first edition of the " Origin of Species " was sold out on the first day, and Darwin, who feared that nobody would ever read it, and who had written to friends who had seen it in proof that, *if* a second edition were ever called for, he would certainly incorporate some of their additions and criticisms, wrote : " I am confounded to find that the whole of the first edition was sold on the first day, and the publishers are calling at once for a second." Edition after edition followed, and then again,

46

to Darwin's almost comic amazement, the book had to be translated into several languages. So little had Darwin expected this that he thought it a very great compliment that a rather eccentric French lady wanted to translate the book into French ; and although her eccentricity was such that she published the book with notes of her own, in which she explained the difficulties that Darwin had been unable to explain, or pointed out that there really were no difficulties at all, Darwin, in his humility, was so pleased with the idea of having a French translation at all that he hardly made any protest !

Nothing is more striking than the humility of this great man—so great that even to-day, when scientists are moving beyond the thought and discovery of Darwin, to us who are not scientists the tyranny of the word " evolution," the almost oppressive force of such phrases as " the struggle for existence," " the survival of the fittest," and so on, make a positive bondage of the intellect—so that to-day Darwin's theory has almost become what the Bible was when the " Origin of Species " was published—a sacred thing that must decide the fate of the League of Nations and the future of the world ! This is an idolatry which Darwin would have been the last to demand for it, seeing that the one thing he desired was always to advance in the service of truth. Yet we must not forget how venomous was the abuse when Darwin first published the book. The fury both of the theological and scientific venom that fell on Darwin has passed so far away that we can hardly imagine it, but it must have been almost unsurpassed in the history of discovery.

Another student of science, Lamarck, had already written something on the same lines as Darwin, and written it rather badly, so that Darwinism, as we call it now, was a little in the position that Spiritualism is to-day. Spiritualism has been associated in people's minds with so much that is false, so much charlatanism, so much swindling, that it is a very bold thing for a man of science to take it seriously at all. It is not a thing that comes new to us ; it is a thing that has been already discredited. So it was with the theory of evolution. Darwin said over and over again—" It is hard to seem even to your friends as though you were insane. It is difficult to persuade even the greatest of my fellow-workers that this theory, this hypothesis, can be anything but a mockery." And as late as 1872, eleven years after his book was published, a scientific society—not a Church—closed its doors to him on the

grounds that the " science " of those of his
chief books which had made his title to
fame, was not science, but a mass of assertions
and absolutely gratuitous hypotheses. " This
kind of publication, and these theories, are a
bad example, which a body that respects
itself cannot encourage." I cannot help being
glad that they were not theologians who said
that, but it must be confessed that theologians
distinguished themselves not a little also.
Some of you will remember that witty,
brilliant, and ignorant speech made by Wilber-
force, Bishop of Oxford, against the theory
of evolution, in the presence of Darwin's
stoutest defender, Huxley ; in which the
Bishop, who was an exceedingly clever man
and a very brilliant speaker, turned aside to
say, seeing Huxley in the audience, that he
understood Mr. Huxley " was not ashamed to
claim an ape for his grandfather." Huxley
replied that he was not in the least ashamed
of having had an ape for a grandfather ;
what would have crushed him with shame
would have been to have had the Bishop of
Oxford for his grandfather !

But Darwin (who was never, in that sense,
a fighter), with that magnanimous humility
that belongs only to the greatest of spirits,
cared profoundly that his hypotheses should
be accepted. He cared chiefly that those

who really knew should believe, that Huxley, Lyell, Agassiz, Asa Gray, and others should believe. This concerned him greatly because he could hardly believe he could be right if such men disagreed with him ; and when Huxley came in at once, with that impulsive generosity—he was as good a friend as a fighter, and more than that one cannot say, for he was a magnificent fighter—when Huxley came in, and, above all, when Lyell came, Darwin's indifference to the criticism of the ignorant, strikes one with amazement. During the whole of his life I think he only once wrote a letter to the newspapers (which were teeming with attacks on him, his morals, his intelligence, his reason), and that letter was written in defence, not of himself, but of a friend. He disregarded altogether the attacks of theologians, not, I think, out of scorn, for Darwin was incapable of scorn, but simply because he felt they spoke of what they did not know, and, on the other hand, he answered the criticisms of even the humblest, the most unknown, the most insignificant critic, if the criticism appeared to him even to attempt to be honest.

When he was questioned about his religious opinions—about all sorts of things on which it seems to us a gross impertinence to question a stranger—every letter was answered, and

50

with such courtesy, such gentleness, such
willingness to assume the best of those who
criticised him, as to compel the admission
that there was something of saintliness in the
life of Darwin. To one who had attacked
him rather vehemently and then apologised,
Darwin wrote : " Do not think I was annoyed
at your letter. I saw that you had been
thinking with animation, and therefore expressed yourself strongly, and so I understood." The next time anybody attacks you
with violence, reflect that they have been
thinking with animation, and therefore they
expressed themselves strongly ! On another
occasion he asks for some more evidence on
a certain point. He says : " Some German
scientists will not believe what I say merely
because the facts strike them as rather
strange." And on another occasion, when
he was trying very hard to get to the bottom
of a rather extraordinary statement, he wrote :
" Somebody wrote to me saying, could I
explain the fact that this year all the beans
had grown on the wrong side. I wrote back
asking for further information, as I did not
perfectly understand what was meant. I
then saw in two newspapers, one in Kent and
one in Yorkshire, a paragraph stating this
remarkable fact, that the beans this year had
all grown on the wrong side. I went to my

gardener and asked him whether he had
heard anything about it. He said, ' Oh, no,
sir, it must be a mistake, for the beans grow
on the wrong side only in leap year, and this
is not leap year.' I then asked him how they
grew in leap year and how in other years,
and I found he knew absolutely nothing of
how they grew at any time. But he stuck
to his belief."

Darwin answered all criticism with infinite
pains, keeping a letter which was perhaps a
mass of abuse, and docketing it if there was
one point in it which was honest and deserved
consideration. And with that profound
humility there goes always a certain ability
to enjoy even what was said against him.
The Bishop of Oxford, undismayed by
Huxley's rebuke, reproduced the substance
of his own speech in an article in the
Quarterly Review. It was an ignorant and
foolish but at the same time very witty attack,
and Darwin spread it among his friends,
asking whether they had seen it, and saying
that they really must read it because the
Bishop had made such splendid fun of him
and his theories.

Of the book itself he always thought that
it was " badly done." Anybody, he says,
who had taken sufficient pains could have
done it. He himself had no particular

talent, except indeed that of industry. When Galton, in his later years, sent him a questionnaire which he had issued to a number of people, he filled up the space beside the question, " What special talents have you ? " with the word " None," and I am quite sure, judging from the whole tenor of his life, that there was no pose in that ; he really did think, as he says, " Anyone with ordinary faculties could have written my book." Elsewhere he says he knows the book is not well done, " but I will not give up the belief that someone who could write better could have made a good book out of the material I have gathered. Some people accuse me of being only a gatherer of facts and having no reasoning power," and here again you find the moderation and humility with which he met every kind of criticism. He says : " I do not think it can be true that I am altogether without reasoning power. The ' Origin of Species ' contains a vast mass of facts, but also many generalisations which have convinced men of not contemptible understanding. I do not think it could have been written by a man wholly without power of reasoning." You might think this is affectation, but if you will read his life by his son you will agree that it is not ; nor is there any suggestion of irony in it. He did

honestly think that "The Origin of Species"
could not have been written by a man wholly
without the power of reasoning. And towards
the end of his life—a life marked by un-
paralleled abuse—he writes this : "My views
have often been grossly misrepresented,
bitterly opposed, and ridiculed, but this has
been generally done, I believe, in good faith.
On the whole, I do not doubt that my works
have been over and over again greatly over-
praised." That a man who had been the
butt of such muddy and unjust abuse could
write at the close of his life that he " believed
it had been generally done in good faith "
fills one with amazement and admiration.
Surely it reaches the high-water mark of
magnanimity. " I cannot say I enjoyed it "
[an attack on him], ". for it made me un-
comfortable for one night, but I have got
quite over it to-day."

Again, when Darwin discovered that Alfred
Russell Wallace had been working on the
same lines as himself, and was perhaps even
readier than himself to publish, the spirit in
which he received that rather shattering news
is beyond our little praise. Wallace had sent
to him an article which he probably desired
to publish, but did not say so. He had asked
Darwin to criticise it, and Darwin found that
in the article was contained the hypothesis

of evolution. Darwin writes to his friend
Lyell that very same day that he got it :
" Your words have come true ; I am fore-
stalled. I never saw a more striking coin-
cidence. If Wallace had my MS. sketch
written out in 1842 " [it was now 1848] " he
could not have made a better abstract. Even
his terms now stand as heads of my chapters.
Please return me the MS., which he does not
say he wished me to publish, but I shall of
course at once write and offer to send to any
journal. So all my originality, whatever it
may amount to, will be smashed, though my
book, if it will ever have any value, will not
be deteriorated, as all the labour consists in
the application of the theory. . . . Wallace
says nothing about publication, but, as I had
not intended to publish any sketch, can I do
so honourably, because Wallace has sent me
an outline of his doctrine ? I would far
rather burn my whole book than that he
should think I had acted in a paltry spirit.
. . . If I could honourably publish, I would
state that I was induced to do so from Wallace
having sent me an outline of my general
conclusions. But I cannot tell whether to
publish now would not be base." And then
he ends, speaking of his disappointment,
" Forgive me, this is a trumpery letter,
influenced by trumpery feeling." We realise

55

that Darwin had been at work on this theory
for nineteen years, and the fact that Wallace had
got his sketch ready first did not necessarily
mean that he was the first man to discover
it. Probably the real priority does belong to
Darwin, but the actual readiness for publication—at least of a short sketch—was Wallace's.
We hardly know which to admire most of
these two great men. Each of them desired
that the other should go forward, and Darwin
in the end paid a fine tribute to Wallace,
who would not hear of Darwin withholding
his own view : " I hope that between us,"
said Darwin, at the end of his life, " there
has never been any ill-feeling. I believe
there has been none in my heart ; I know
there has been none in yours."

That is how he met the scientist. How
did he meet the theologian ? As I have said,
he did not answer *merely* abusive attacks of
theologians. When people, humble individuals, wrote to ask him whether he believed
in God, whether he believed in Christ, and
so on, he answered, broadly speaking, that
he could not know, that he was, in the real
sense of the word, " agnostic " ; he did not
know what was the First Cause or whether
there was a God. I think Darwin worshipped
God under one of his most fundamental
aspects, since he worshipped truth. " I cannot

56

write on a theological question," he said,
" because I have not thought deeply enough
to justify me in writing," and elsewhere—
" I can no longer read poetry with any pleasure.
Music means nothing to me. There is a certain
side of life to which I have become deaf and
blind. My mind seems to be only a kind of
machine for grinding out great generalisations
about masses of facts. How can I judge
where I do not experience ? Had I to live
over again, I think I should give a little time
every day to reading poetry or to hearing
music. But it is too late ; I must go on as
I am." How many of us are so unwilling to
judge where we neither know nor understand ?
There is in this intellectual asceticism of
Darwin, which sacrificed poetry, music, everything, to the pursuit of his one scientific
passion, something very like the asceticism
of St. Francis, who has no wife, no family,
no home, because the one passion of his life
excluded all the rest. And when I read of
Darwin saying sadly—" If I were to live
again I should give a little time every day
to poetry and music," I am reminded of
St. Francis, who rushed out in the night to
make figures of wife and children out of the
snow. But wisdom is justified of all her
children. If Darwin lost an experience he
did not dogmatise on what he lost. If

St. Francis lost something, how much more he gained! And if a great enthusiasm for a great end makes a saint, then Darwin stands no lower than St. Francis of Assisi. He worshipped God under the great aspect of truth.

"I always note down immediately," he said, "a fact that tells against me, for I have noticed that the memory willingly lets go that which it does not desire to retain." You who have engaged in controversy, do you not "note down immediately the fact" which tells on your side? Have you ever discovered, as did this man with his saint-like devotion to truth, that the memory "willingly lets go" the facts that tell against you? "There is no man in the world who so eagerly publishes his mistakes," said Huxley, "as Darwin. There is no one who more quickly throws open to the world the facts that tell against him. I believe that if to-day he were to find some shattering instance which broke to pieces the work of his life, he would put it down for publication to-morrow."

We ask, did Darwin believe in Christ? I think if Darwin ever committed himself to a denial of any kind, it was a denial of the personality of God. And personality is—so Christians believe—an attribute of God. How many of the attributes of God do we deny?

58

When we proclaim aloud in our churches every week that God is a jealous God, which of his attributes are we then denying ? When we starve other nations, are we not denying the Fatherhood of God ? When we preach that God is the source and origin of disease, which of the attributes of God are we denying ? We believe in a personal God ; but is it so great a thing to believe in a personal God and deny that God is Truth ? Did not the whole of organised Christianity deny that, when it persecuted Darwin and sought to prove him a liar, simply because people were afraid to face what he had to teach ?

God is infinitely more merciful than we, and, if we worship him under any of his great aspects—Beauty, or Love, or Truth, or in the person of our Lord Jesus Christ, God accepts us all. If he were to wait for a worshipper who should " believe in " all his attributes, if he were to wait for a man and woman who should know all that God is and worship all, he would have to wait long ! Who knows all of God ? Which of us has not denied God under some aspect or other ? And surely the aspect of truth is a very terrible one to deny. I cannot lay down the life of Darwin without remembering that Jesus himself said : " If any man blaspheme against the Son of Man (that was, against

59

himself) it shall be forgiven him, but he that blasphemeth against the Holy Spirit it shall not be forgiven him." Why? Because so long as you will not admit the truth, so long as you put evil for good, and good for evil, so long as you set truth for a lie—and who shall say the Churches did not do so when Darwin sought to teach them?—you are in a damnable state of mind. This is not a merely intellectual error; it is a state of mind which makes the kingdom of God impossible to you, and you are " in danger of damnation."

THE LAWS OF LIFE

" Henceforth I call you not servants ; for the
servant knoweth not what his Lord doeth. But I have
called you friends ; for all things that I have heard
of my Father I have made known unto you."—

John xvi, 15.

OUR Lord calls us his friends, not only
because we love him, but because we
know him. Every great movement of the
human spirit is meant to be a revelation to
us of the nature and purpose of God, and
every nation, every race, every century, has
added to the religious experience of the
world, and has made known to us more and
more of the nature of God. All this knowledge was summed up and set forth to us so
that we could understand it, when God himself
came to this world in our Lord Jesus Christ.
" I call you not servants, but I have called
you friends ; because all things that I have
heard of my Father, I have made known
unto you." But that knowledge is not ended
with the death of Christ, as he reminded us
again and again on that last evening of his
life ; it was to be progressive ; the Holy
Spirit would lead us into all truth, so that,

61

though with the coming of our Lord, we are made no longer servants but friends, the revelation is still not complete: " I have many things to say unto you, but ye cannot bear them now." Our knowledge of our Father in Heaven is to grow with every movement of the human spirit, and every advance in knowledge should be to those that love God, a revelation of his nature and purpose.

Perhaps the greatest revelation which has come to the world since the death of Christ is that which seems to cut off the modern man and woman from the man and woman of two or three hundred years ago—the great advance in scientific knowledge, which has altered our whole way of looking at life, and has seemed to some to destroy the very foundations of their faith. But science has come to us with a revelation of the nature of the world in which we live, and since that world was made and is governed by God, the revelation of science should have been recognised by us as a revelation of the nature of God himself.

That knowledge has been a revelation of unfailing law. That which men observed in the past as so many isolated phenomena has now become related as a great principle. The greatest of modern scientists, the man whose work cuts off the modern from the

mediæval world, Sir Isaac Newton, observed
only what every man had observed, but he
observed with the insight of genius ; from the
fall of an apple he generalised the law by
which the universe is governed, and realised
and taught to us that these laws are statements
of fact without exception. We use words
rather clumsily, and scientific law is of course
not a law that these things must be, or shall
be, under sanction : they are statements
that these things *are*, and a scientific law is a
statement of fact *without exception*. It has
been pointed out how often this or that
beautiful theory has been broken down by
the discovery of one single inconvenient
fact. For if there is one inconvenient fact,
the law has been wrongly stated, misunderstood, or perhaps is not a law at all. The
scientist, with that humility which belongs
to those who love truth, is very " agnostic "
in laying down the law, is very doubtful
whether any law has been finally stated : but
the thing of which he is certain and of which
he has made us certain is that " the world
is lawful to the core." The laws we may not
yet perfectly have stated ; many of them
we have not even begun to understand ;
but we realise that the world is lawful to the
core, that to these laws there is no exception.
They never fail, they never swerve, they

never cease to operate. By them not only
the fall of an apple but the motion of the
stars is governed, and the great physical
forces which we are learning to harness to
the use of man are subject to laws and move
in obedience to laws which never fail.

Before that revelation of the world all minds,
perhaps, except the very greatest, were
smitten by a sense of impotence. The iron
rigidity of law from which no man could
escape, which no prayers could avert, seemed
to turn the world into a machine.

> " Streams do not curb their pride
>   The just man not to entomb,
>   Nor lightnings turn aside
>   To give his virtues room.
> The world is what it is, for all our dust and din."*

In the presence of that great discovery, that
the whole universe moves in obedience to
unalterable law—the spirit of man was
paralysed.

But we soon began to realise that in fact
the existence of unalterable law is not
paralysing but liberating, and that if the
law were *not* unfailing, we should be helpless
before its operation, and the world would
become chaos again. If the law of gravitation
did not always operate, if there were times

* *Empedocles on Etna.*—Matthew Arnold.

when the world was governed by some other
law, if the writ of God did not run through
the universe, we could not co-operate with it.
It is by understanding the law, by stating it
truly, and by co-operating with it, that man
has learned to control, and in a sense even to
govern the physical world he lives in. Not
until the law was understood came that
great advance in applied science which has
seemed to make us gods indeed. As long as
we conceived that the fall of an apple was
only the fall of an apple, science was half
paralysed ; but when we understood that
every particle of matter is governed by the
same law, when we realised that that law
could be stated and understood and, when
understood, we could know with absolute
certainty that it knows no exception, then
there came that great advance in applied
science, that liberation of the human spirit,
that seeming defiance of the law ; which
only means that we have understood it so
well that we can co-operate with it and make
ourselves lords of the physical world. A man
who learns to fly is not defying the law of
gravitation : he is only understanding it
and the laws of motion and other laws so
perfectly, that he is able to co-operate with
them. And if he falters and falls, if his
machine comes crashing to the ground, he

does not suppose that the laws in which he trusted have ceased to operate. He knows that whatever becomes of him, these laws cannot have failed, and that it is only because our understanding of them is still incomplete, that we cannot perfectly control the great forces of the universe. It is in proportion as we understand them that we can co-operate with them. All our power would be taken from us if nature were not what we have sometimes called her accusingly—relentless. If relentless Nature ever could relent, if the law could ever be broken, if these great forces should operate by caprice, that liberation of the human spirit which comes from co-operating with what we understand and can rely upon would become impossible.

There is a sense of the poetry of law in modern science which is almost intoxicating to the human spirit. Just the fall here and there of some material object—that is nothing : but the law of gravitation which holds the world in its place and rules the motions of the stars—that is eternal poetry, and as it is formulated to us by our teachers, there surges across our sense the music of the spheres. We realise that what we call " law " is indeed a divine harmony, which, understood, teaches us something of the nature and the purpose of our God.

66

Is it perhaps because religious people, instead of realising that all truth must be of God and tell us something about God, fought against the truth as though it were an enemy—as though between the God of Christianity and the God of Truth there could be war—is it for that reason that we have so little translated into our conception of God this certainty, this unfailing unalterable law which is reflected in the universe he made? If we had welcomed that truth, as Christ forewarned us we should always welcome the truth, could we not have carried over into the law of the spiritual world this great certainty, and calmness, and liberation of the spirit, which comes when we know the laws of the physical world? Our God is the Father of lights in whom is no variableness neither shadow cast by turning; and if he made this law of the world, has he not also made the unfailing, unswerving, unchangeable spiritual laws which we see in operation every day, as our forefathers saw in operation the law of gravitation? These laws run through the universe and the spiritual power by which our Lord healed the sick, raised the dead, cast out devils, calmed the storm, is still here with us, surging around us, operating in the lives of every one of us and every day. But we have not the audacity to generalise those experiences into a great law—the purpose of God.

But surely if God is thus God of the physical world, he cannot be an altogether different God in the spiritual world. Why dare we not assume of him that stability that we find in the world he made ? Is it perhaps because we fought against that revelation of truth, that we still think of our Father in heaven as a capricious, uncertain, unreliable force, that is sometimes love and sometimes not, sometimes almighty, and sometimes not ; so that there is in our religious life very little of the courage and faith of the great scientists ? I speak only of the greatest but there is surely in the temper of the true scientist, a certainty, a courage, and a humility which are profoundly religious. Because his God is a God of truth and law, his spirit is upright in the presence of that law, with which he can work as Christ also worked. In the personality of Christ there is also this sense of power and force and courage. There is no faltering in his spiritual purpose ; there is no doubt, no hesitation. There is sometimes a shrinking from the pain and sacrifice involved, but there is no uncertainty, there is no doubt, there is none of that paralysing sense of impotence which characterises the religious of to-day. Christ, greater than the Newtons or the Darwins of the physical world, so perfectly understood the spiritual laws and the spiritual forces governed by those laws, so understood the purpose and the will of God, that at every step he controlled and commanded those forces, and dominated the spiritual world as our scientists to-day are learning to dominate the physical world.

And not the physical as opposed to the spiritual, but both at once. It was not only the forces of love and hate and courage and fear and sin and righteousness which Christ understood, but the human body with its sickness which he healed, its untimely death which he could overcome. It was the world, the physical world which he governed at once with the spiritual world. For indeed, there is no difference and no distinction. If we had understood that, should we ever have dreamed of stopping short at the bounds of the physical world, and said of the great laws of God, " thus far and no farther " ? Up to here, we think, the world is governed by law but, pass beyond that into the region of the spirit, and there is no certainty and no law, and God is a capricious, perhaps a beneficent tyrant, but capricious, uncertain, unreliable, whom we can only beseech to be merciful, hoping that he may hear our

F

prayers ; not that God of the scientist who hideth not himself, whose laws are there for all to understand.

In the spiritual world, cannot we attain to the certainty and power which the scientist has given to the human spirit in the world which we call the physical world ? All around us these spiritual laws are operating. All the time we see people transformed by love, healed by faith, restored by hope, corrupted by hate, destroyed by cruelty. But when we see one healed by faith, we think this is a strange exception, a remarkable phenomenon not to be counted upon ; to be received with thankfulness indeed, but not to be generalised from as an instance of a great law running through the universe. Yet this spiritual force whose operation we recognise here and there, which sometimes heals the sick, which sometimes solves our problems, this spiritual force is always there. If we would so understand it, we could co-operate with it, working together with God in his universe, so that the spiritual world should be ours as the physical world is ours. With what faltering hands we touch the levers of those terrible forces ! With what dim eyes we peer at the stars ! " Oh that I knew where I might find him ! " we cry, and all the while God answers " I am not a God which hideth

myself." In the presence of the greatest
material advance the world has ever made,
in the presence of physical forces so tremendous
that they seem almost to paralyse the human
spirit, we stand in doubt and wonder, not
knowing which way to turn ; and all the
while the world is instinct with spiritual
powers infinitely greater and more wonderful
in their operation than those physical forces
which for centuries we have studied with
such concentrated care.

And because we stop short at the physical
discovery, is it not true to say that even the
physical advance has turned to our
destruction ? I speak of our having learned
to command the physical world, and in a
sense that is true ; but is it not also true
that long before the war began, the spirits
of men were troubled, anxious, almost
paralysed with a sense that the very greatness of their discoveries had recoiled upon
them, that those inventions which should
have set free human beings have almost
crushed them, so that our industrial revolution
which was to have brought some leisure and
joy and ease into the world has ended by
making of a man the slave instead of the
master of his machine ? In the presence of
that vast and complex structure which we
call modern civilisation, the spirit of man

is almost crushed under the burden of its own knowledge and its own powers. When science goes further and arms the nations with an armour under the weight of which they stagger, is it not again because, though we have understood so well what scientific truth has meant, we have not dared to make the next step and go on from the truth of the physical world to the truth of God who made the world? "The Holy Spirit shall lead you," said our Lord, "into all truth"; and when knowledge came and our Father revealed himself indeed, we shrank from the revelation in terror unworthy of Christian people. We shrank from it, and therefore we lost the power and the insight which Christ possessed to make that further step, from the knowledge of the laws of the physical universe to the knowledge of those mighty forces beyond, behind, above, around us, which should have made us masters indeed of the world in which we live.

Is it, perhaps, possible that out of the very anguish and darkness of the world, out of the very depth of our economic misery, our industrial struggle, our international strife, we, who cannot live without God, who dare not, who cannot face life if these terrific physical forces are all—may it not be that out of the very heart of this misery we shall

be shocked into a realisation of the greatness
of the soul of man, and those still greater
spiritual powers which dominate the physical
world ? "Greater works than these shall
ye do," said he who healed the sick and raised
the dead. His promise no more fails than
do his laws. It is we who have failed, it
is we who turned our backs upon the truth
in fear. But "greater works than these
shall ye do." "Henceforth, I call you not
servants but I have called you friends. For
the servant knoweth not what his Master
doeth." Out of the heart of physical conflict,
in the face of physical forces so terrible that
we who live here at home cannot even imagine
their potentiality for destruction ; out of the
very sense of helplessness in the presence of
so vast a conflict, out of the crushing burden
laid upon our spirits by the vast and complex
structure of modern civilisation, we shall
take courage at last to affirm the greatness of the spiritual law. We shall apply
ourselves to the understanding of that law
with the same courage and the same
confidence, the same certainty in the unfailing
operation of God's love, as became us when
we studied the laws of science. If we had
studied the law of God, in the light of Christ's
love, and in the hearts of one another, in
the operation of the laws of science and in

the movements of the human spirit, with a passionate love of truth, with unflinching sincerity of purpose, with courage and with assurance, by now what should we not have attained ? It is not yet too late. Let us take courage. There has never been a time when men were willing to sacrifice more or when they felt more urgently the need of this affirmation of spiritual freedom. Our God is a God without variableness or shadow cast by turning. Let us co-operate with his great purpose unafraid, only seeking to learn from life the secret of God's law. And we shall know that that love which governs our relations with our friends, that faith which can heal the human body, are God's writs running through the universe, which never fail, which never change. The spirit of man will be liberated indeed when he studies the law of God ; so that working together with God we may do greater works than Christ himself. "I call you friends," said our Saviour, and we reply, "Oh, Lord thy word endureth for ever in heaven. Thou hast laid the foundations of the earth and it endureth. I see that all things come to an end, but thy commandments are exceeding broad."

ST. JOAN OF ARC

TO some of you, I believe, Joan of Arc is almost as remote a figure [as our King Arthur. Did she ever exist, or is she a mere legend ? Certainly she existed ; and in fact there is no other saint in the world who is more easy to know personally. She did not write anything ; she could neither write nor read ; but when she was brought to trial at Rouen the questions that were put to her (which cover almost the whole of her life), and the answers she made to them, were all taken down by reporters in the court, and some part of these questions and answers has come down to us in the very form and language that Joan of Arc used. The whole of the examination has come down to us translated into Latin by the Court Officer. Only a short passage is preserved in the original French, but even in the translation into mediæval Latin we can catch the voice of Joan of Arc. We can watch how day after day her spirits rose or sank. We can read the very soul of this woman, catch her very accents, as day after day she answered her

enemies on almost every passage of her life.
And then, after they had killed her, twenty-
five years later, there was another trial to
rehabilitate her memory, when all her friends
—all the great soldiers who had followed her
in war—the friends she had known in
her little village home—her relations and
little school companions—were called to tell
what they knew about Joan of Arc. The
report of that trial has also come down to us.
And although we have to make allowance,
in the first case, for the translation into Latin,
and in the second for the fact that the people
who spoke for her were nearly all her friends,
still it is true to say that we get a unique
portrait of a living, breathing woman, and
can know more about Joan of Arc's mind and
soul than perhaps about any other saint in
the calendar, who left, like her, no written
record.

The whole of her public career lasted just
over one year. In thirteen months, this
uneducated girl, this child of a peasant father
and mother, without education, without position, without wealth, changed the face of
Europe. She saved her country. Incidentally,
I think any historian would admit that she
also saved ours, because we were engaged in
a war with France, which was ruining us.
She introduced into Europe, through France,

the great country of ideas, that spirit of nationality which was then quite new ; for in those days one town would fight another, just as to-day one country fights another, and the sense of France as one great nation was given to her by Joan of Arc. When she died, France was a nation. If some of you say you " do not believe in nationality," I would remind you that nationality must come before internationality, and that you cannot have a federation, or a league of peoples, until the peoples themselves are conscious of their individual existence, and their individual service to the world. And that great step forward in European history was due, more perhaps than to any other one person, to this young peasant girl of eighteen years of age.

Let me remind you of the details of her life. She was born in the middle of the Hundred Years War, about 1412 or 1413. When she was about thirteen or fourteen years of age, she tells us, she began to hear the voices of three saints directing her earthly life. And if you are inclined to think that people who hear voices directing them must be hysterical, foolish, and mistaken, remember that the only phenomenon in history which closely resembles the way in which Joan of Arc's life was guided by the voices of her saints,

77

is found in the life of Socrates. I know of no other great saint whose life was guided continually by the voice of some spirit which he believed to be outside himself, which spoke to him continually as though it were the voice of God. If it be a madness to be guided by voices such as those which guided Socrates and Joan of Arc, I wish that some of us could lose our senses also.

Joan believed that she heard these voices, and that they told her first of all " to be good," and afterwards to go and save her country. She refused to do this. She had no influence. She was utterly unknown. She thought it was impossible. But the first part of the advice she took. And because she was, within the limits of her power, utterly faithful, she heard ever more and more insistently the command of God to save her country ; and at last she set out.

Now when she set out, France was almost at the lowest point of her fortunes. The English were holding about two-thirds of France, and were advancing further and further south, to Orleans. Orleans stands on the north side of the curve of the great river Loire—the only city north of the Loire that held out. The French were retreating further and further south before the English army. Remember this, for it is easy to think of

Joan of Arc as coming in on the flood tide.
That would be mistaken. She came just
when the Dauphin was abandoning the part
of France he held, and retreating still farther
to the south. Joan went to the nearest
military town and asked the governor to give
her a horse and escort to the Dauphin. At
first he jeered, but when she had been there
a little while he stopped laughing at her and
gave her a horse. She went to the Dauphin
and said, " I have come to help you, and I
shall prove it by relieving the town of Orleans."
The Dauphin had a superstitious feeling that
perhaps Joan would bring him luck. I do
not think he thought anything more serious
than that. So after much hesitation and after
having had her examined by a large number
of clergy in order to be quite sure that she
was perfectly orthodox, he said she might go.
She tells us in her trial that the Prince said
to her, " Before we believe that you come
from God, you must give us a sign." She
said, " My sign will be that I raise the
siege of Orleans." But they said that
would not do, and after a long while, she
says, God did give her a sign. We do not
know what it was, but it convinced them.
The judges said, " What did you do when
God gave you the sign ? " She said, " I
went into church and thanked God for

79

delivering me from those clergy who argued with me ! "

Joan went to Orleans with a small force. At the end of about eight days the English army was in full retreat, and the city of Orleans was saved. Joan of Arc immediately went to the Dauphin and said, " You must now set out for the city of Rheims, where you shall be crowned," because until the king of France was crowned with the sacred oil he was not regarded by the people as king at all. That is where Joan's "sanctified commonsense" came in ! The thing the English had neglected to do—to crown their little baby king with this anointing of the sacred oil—was just exactly the thing the Dauphin ought to do at once, in order that the people might recognise that God had made him king of France. But between Orleans and Rheims the whole of the country was held by the English. The Dauphin therefore said to Joan, " I do not think you can have noticed that the whole of this country is in the hands of the English, and they have all the towns between here and Rheims ! " " I have noticed it," she said, " and I make nothing of it. The great thing is to start ! If you are not there first the king of England will be. Let us start ! " At last the Dauphin gave way to her impetuous faith, and they set out for Rheims. As they went city after city sent its keys, to lay them at the feet of the Dauphin, and even those which made some show of resistance, when the Maid of France advanced, opened their gates to her.

When they reached Rheims that city itself also opened its gates to receive the king, and he was crowned in the Cathedral with the sacred oil. The first great step in the salvation of France was accomplished. After that, the Dauphin naturally thought he might sit down and rest a little. He said he was sure Joan was very tired, and would she not like to rest too? " Rest ? " she said, " The English are in Paris ! How can we rest ? " " But Paris is a very strong city," he said, "and a great many English are there, and when the English shout ' Hurrah ! ' all the French soldiers run away." And it was a fact that, before Joan of Arc came, they did so, so utterly demoralised were they.

" I have only got a year," said Joan. " Let us go to Paris." Any soldier here will agree that Joan of Arc was absolutely right. She had so far never known defeat. But there was not a moment to delay. It was not now the French who fled from the English, but the English who were terror-stricken by the Maid of France. They thought the girl was

a witch, and if the French army had moved
on from Rheims to Paris we know from actual
report what Joan of Arc guessed, that the
people were in a panic, and that almost
certainly they also would have opened their
gates to the king. But at this point the
clergy and the politicians were too strong for
Joan. They thought that things were really
going too fast. It simply took their breath
away to go galloping about France like that !
Nearly a hundred years the war had dragged
on, and it looked as though this girl was going
to put an end to it in a few weeks! " At any
rate," she said, " let me go on." So she
went alone to Paris. But she was unsup-
ported by the king, who should have been
in the field himself, at the head of his army.
The guns were never brought into action at
all. The English had been as swift as she
was, and had profited by the delay to fortify
the city and call up extra troops. When
Joan of Arc appeared before the gates of
Paris it was already too late. For a day she
cried her men on to the assault ; for a day
they fought outside Paris. When night came
on she retired to rest, and when the morning
broke, and she was about to take the field
again, she got a message from the king to
say she was to return at once. She threw
herself on to her horse and went to the king

to entreat him to allow her to continue the
assault on Paris. He refused. She still was
undaunted, and since he would not give her
permission, she went without it. She turned
her horse's head to Paris, only to find that
the king had destroyed the bridge over the
river by which she could have returned.
Then indeed despair for a moment seized
her. She hung up her armour in the little
chapel of St. Denis, the patron saint of
France, and went back to the king. She
began at once to ask what they should do
next. The great soldiers, the great leaders of
that age, men of European reputation, all of
them desired that in any case Joan should
go with them. They said, "There are
thousands who will not stir unless she is
with us." But they were not allowed to have
her. I do not know what those politicians
were about, or whether they found it impossible to believe that this girl was directed
by God himself—impossible to believe that
she could achieve the impossible—but, week
after week, month after month, they frittered
away her prestige, her strength and her power.
At last, when she heard that the little city of
Compiégne northwards of Paris, was about
to fall she went to defend it. The day after
her entry she made a sally against the English,
and as her little band met them, Joan was

surrounded and driven off the causeway into the marsh; and at last she who, to her eternal honour, was always first in the advance and last in the retreat, was separated from her men and taken prisoner by the English. We English have need to feel ashamed of our record with Joan of Arc, but upon my word I do not think her own countryfolk have very much to boast of! They sold her to the English king, and from the beginning to the end of her imprisonment not one effort was made by the people to whom she had given freedom, by the king to whom she had given his crown, to release her from those who were bent on her destruction.

Joan of Arc was a prisoner. The first thing she did was to refuse to give any promise not to escape. She could not conceive that the king to whom she had given a kingdom would really make no effort to save her, and how would she feel when her friends came to rescue her if she had given her parole? She was bound to refuse, and looking round she said, "Remember—if I escape, I shall not have broken my word, for I give no word." They said, "Would you escape from prison if it were against the will of God?" "No, not if it were against the will of God." "Not if you saw the door open?" one asked with a sneer. "In the name of God," she an-

swered, " if I saw the door open, I should
think it *was* the will of God!" Then they
accused her of having tried to escape before.
" Why, yes," she said. " I never was in
any prison yet that I did not try to escape
from." And she added, " Is that not the
right of prisoners ? " Prisoners indeed have
no rights but this one, the right to escape if
they can, and that right Joan of Arc would
never abandon. But realise what her deter-
mination meant! Had she consented to
promise not to escape, she would have been
put into a political prison, she would have been
allowed some kind of decency, in surroundings
that were not altogether horrible. But because she refused to give that promise, she
was left in the hands of the English army.
This girl, whose nature was so pure and lovely
that, the soldiers tell us, one after another,
no thought of impurity could enter their
minds in her presence—this girl for eight
weeks rose and slept, ate and lived, suffered
and prayed in the presence of British men
at arms. Not for one instant was she out
of their presence. There may be saints who
have endured a more exquisite torture than
this ; if there are, I do not know them.
With actual danger of violation, with no
privacy and no quiet—any man or woman
being allowed to come and stare at the witch

who had been caught at last—at the mercy
of her enemies, her courage never failed, her
conviction never wavered that God would
save her. Her loyalty to the king whom she
had crowned never for an instant faltered.
Day after day she was brought before her
tormentors, who wanted to extract from her
something to disgrace the king of France.
She said, "I shall tell you nothing. If I
have done wrong, it is my fault. I alone am
responsible."

"Did no one tell you to wear the dress of
a man?"

"No one told me," she said. "If it is
wrong, it is I who have done it."

Then they said, "Do you not think it
wrong to dress yourself like a man?"

"In the name of God, why do you occupy
yourselves with such trifles? It is a matter
of no moment to you how I dress. When I
live among men it is more decent that I dress
like a man."

They said, "Would you take a woman's
dress if we allowed you to hear mass?"

She had a great desire to hear mass. She
hesitated and said, "I would take a woman's
dress, but I beseech you to let me hear it as
I am. This does not offend God."

There is a hideous terror behind this
trifling question of the dress of Joan of Arc,

for, for a woman to dress as a man was a
heresy, and they wanted to prove that she
was a heretic and a witch.

Question after question was put to her, and
she answered with such childlike directness,
with such divine simplicity, that they could
not entrap her.

" Do you believe yourself," they said, " to
be in a state of salvation ? " Those of you
who know anything of mediæval theology
know that that question was one almost
impossible to answer without heresy. Even
the very judges began to protest that such
a question ought not to be put, but before
they could intervene she had answered :
" If I am, God keep me so," she said, " and
if I am not, God make me so."

Convict her they could not, but condemn
her they could, and when they found they
could get nothing out of her they decided to
pronounce the sentence.

She was taken out to die in the market-
place of Rouen. They sent a priest to
preach to her before she died, and in that
last hour, when she was on the verge of
despair, with death before her eyes—for the
faggot and scaffold were there as she stood—
at that last hour, when she heard the preacher
turn aside from his talk to her to attack her
king, who had not lifted a finger to save her—

87

" You lie," she cried. " My Prince is the noblest and best soul in Christendom ! "

And then all the horror of death came upon her. Throughout her career we can see how strong she was, how full of life, how quickly healed from a wound, how immune from fatigue ; and all that young and glorious vitality suddenly made death seem intolerable. She had never believed she would die. She had counted with the same certainty on her king delivering her as he might have counted on her. And then, when neither the heaven opened, nor her friends came to save her, suddenly that dauntless spirit for a moment quailed. She cried out that if she had been wrong she would recant. A piece of paper was thrust into her hand with a form of recantation which she could not read, and she put a mark on it to show that she accepted ; and she was taken back to prison.

We know that after three days Joan of Arc was found once more in her man's dress, a sign that she had, as they said, " relapsed into sin." When they questioned her, we find that she no longer believed that her Voices had led her astray. " It is I," she said, " who have failed. I never meant to say my Voices deceived me. They never have deceived me. I signed that form because I was afraid of death. And my Voices have

come to me in prison, and have reproached
me for my great treason. They have told
me I ought not to have been afraid, that I
have indeed perjured myself when I said
God did not send me, *for in truth He did
send me.*"

"Do your own people now believe God
sent you?" they asked her.

"I do not know," she said, "but whether
they believe it or not, God did send me."

So they condemned her again, and once
more she was taken out into the market-place
to die. They had never meant that she
should escape. Whatever she had said or
done, they would have entrapped her. So
she was led out again to the market-place of
Rouen; but this time there was no cry, no
failure. In the words of Mr. Andrew Lang—
"She listened patiently; her warfare was
over, and it is on record that her judges
wept. They had no pity, but they had
sentiment." She climbed the ladder of the
scaffold, and as the flames rose around her
she warned the priests who stood near her
to stand a little farther off because they were
in danger. They heard her calling upon her
saints as the flames mounted, and then at
last, with a great cry of "Jesus!" she gave
up her spirit. That the world might have
no record of her of whom the world was not

worthy, the people gathered her ashes together and threw them into the Seine.

Only the other day Joan of Arc was canonised. For five hundred years no recognition was given to this most childlike and most lovely saint, Joan of Arc, to whom the death even of her enemies was a tragedy, who time after time would succour the wounded and dying English as gladly as she succoured the wounded and dying French. She has had no official recognition till now, but in our hearts she has long had her altar, and we only desire that we may share even a very little of that heroic spirit which, without resources, without wealth, without power or influence, simply by following the Voice of God, saved her country from the crucifixion of war—and our country also.

THE FEAR OF FREEDOM

" Thou that destroyest the temple, and buildest it in three days, save thyself and come down from the cross. Likewise also the chief priests mocking said among themselves with the scribes, he saved others ; himself he cannot save.

" Let Christ the King of Israel descend now from the cross that we may see and believe."—Mark xv, 29-32.

I HAVE been speaking lately about Christ as a friend but did not dwell on one of the loveliest qualities of his friendship, because it is a quality which he showed to all human beings and not to his friends only. It is the quality of reverence for a person's reserves, for their freedom, for their personality, which human beings do not always show, even to those they love best. Indeed, perhaps they show it least—unless they are very careful—to the people they love best.

Our Lord never forced people to do what they thought was not right, or to do what they could not see a reason for doing ; or even to believe in him. I suppose most of us feel that in that first great scene in his life when he was tempted—what form the temptation took, what lies behind the dramatic narrative,

91

we do not know—that one of the things that he was tempted to do was to use his amazing moral and spiritual power to strike people's imaginations, to do something extraordinary, to use some astonishing power in order to force himself at once on their notice. He was only a carpenter—a person without position and without wealth—and his one advantage was his great spiritual power. No doubt the temptation that came to him was to use that power in order so to strike the imagination of the world as to give him an instant advantage in dealing with it. He put that on one side, and evidently he put it on one side for ever. For it is perfectly clear that our Lord dreaded impressing people by some mighty work in such a way as to silence their doubts and to stun their imagination. He saw people beginning to follow him because he did mighty works or miracles. He began to be reluctant to work them. He seemed to withdraw himself. The power which Christians have regarded—and rightly —as one of the proofs of his greatness, he was anxious not to use in that way. He reproached people for being so easily impressed : he was sensitive for their freedom and judgment, for what he wanted was a moral judgment. He was afraid of their regarding a miracle as a kind of conjuring trick and thinking of him as a magician. He was so respectful to their intellectual freedom and their moral judgment that he would not allow them, if he could help it and so far as he could help it, to be stunned into acquiescence, to have their imaginations so seized that they forgot the deeper things that he was talking about. He did not want to gain their assent or their belief in him by any kind of spectacular advertisement, by any kind of conjuring trick.

This is, however, a very subtle temptation to most of us. We like very often to capture people's imagination or to violate their freedom, to win their judgment by some ways that we hardly realise are a little illegitimate, or not quite fair to the person we are trying to convince. Still we do realise as a principle that people should be free to judge, to judge for themselves, even to make their own mistakes. It was better for Judas to reject Christ than to accept him because he could exercise some magical power. It was better for Peter to fail than for our Lord so to hold him up and coerce his moral judgment that he ceased to be a free person at all.

Parents—especially mothers—know that it is one of the most difficult things to let a child tumble and risk hurting itself. Every moment she wants to run after it and catch it, so that it shall be safe. But she lets it risk hurting

93

itself because it must learn to run. It is not even a risk, it is a certainty. It *will* hurt itself; it *will* fall down. You have to let it fall sometimes. You have to let it make its own mistakes, and the mother who is always catching her child up out of danger is not really the one who is wisest or most loving, any more than are parents who, when their children grow up, will not give them freedom, will not allow them to have a chance to make their own mistakes, who hold them back by the power of their authority, or their purse, or by that still more dread power of their love and gratitude. It is not the most loving parent who will not give his son or his daughter a chance to make their own mistakes.

When you bring children into the world you run a risk, but it is not the people who love children who abstain from having them because they are afraid the children may hurt them, or may hurt themselves, or may do what is wrong when they grow up. I talk of the risk, but again it is not a risk; it is a certainty. You choose it because you love children, because you love them so much that you are prepared to suffer what their freedom may inflict on you. The father who lets the prodigal son take his portion and go away and spend it, would, I suppose, seem to some people very unwise; but he was not.

94

I have known rescue-workers tell me sometimes they have to let a girl go. They have done everything in their power to keep her, but the point comes when they must allow her to go, and let her come back of herself if she will. That costs something! But they are surely right. We are learning more and more how reluctant we should be to coerce, but the more we love people the harder it is, for love has a terrible power of coercion.

We can by appealing to love, by appealing to gratitude, by appealing to the rights of a parent or the rights of a friend, make our love a tyranny. Years ago a very witty play called " The Tyranny of Tears " was put on the stage. In it a wife exercised a tyranny over her husband by bursting into tears every time she wanted anything. That is the sort of thing some people do over and over again. They tell you how terribly they are grieving, how much they are hurt. They are not angry, but they are pained, and really the person who is pained is almost impossible! Consequently, you give way, but with such a sense of outrage, such a sense of resentment, because that person has used the most sacred power on earth not to guide you, not to inspire you, not to help you, but to force you, to coerce you ; and that is a thing love should never do.

So if we are wise, we try to set our friends and our children free, and we know that that freedom is the mark of nobility in human nature. It is our freedom to give love or to withhold love, to serve or to withhold our services, that makes our help and love worth anything. Otherwise, what is it? It is not possible to force love : but if it were, who would value it? It is because someone *gives* it to you that it is so lovely. That is why a child's love is so indescribably touching; because a child has no reason whatever to show love for you except that it really does love. Freedom makes both the happiness and the nobility of human beings.

Yet there is no gift of which Humanity is more afraid than its own freedom. There were slaves who fought against their own enfranchisement in the American Civil War. There were women who refused their political freedom in the fight for the suffrage. Everywhere, where people are enslaved, or oppressed, or subject, there will be among them those who prefer that state of being, to freedom. So, among human beings, there are many who desire that they should be coerced by God. They want to know what they are to do, what they are to think, what they are to be. I remember a clergyman once said to me that I should not complain so much about the jack-in-office attitude of some of the clergy if I knew how hard it was to escape it. He said people come to him and say, " What shall I think about so-and-so ? " and he says, " What *do* you think ? " They say, " Oh, I want you to tell me ! " And one is tempted to say, " Think this, or that, or the other, only go away ! "

The attitude of mind which says, " Please tell me what to think, what to be, what to aim at, what to do," is the slave still lingering in the human heart. It is the slavish desire to escape responsibility, to escape the dangers of freedom, to escape the risk of making mistakes, which asks, " Why does not God prevent war ? Why does not God reveal himself so that I can understand ? If he is speaking to me, why does he not *make* me hear ? Why does he not *make* me love him ? *Force* me to understand ? If he is comprehensible why has not he given me the power with which to understand ? " It sounds very reasonable, and I suppose there is no more universal charge against God than the fact that he does not force us, will not work the miracle which would coerce our judgment, any more than Christ would come down from the cross in order that those who stood around should see and believe.

" Let Christ the King of Israel descend

from the cross *that we may see and believe.*"
Well, if he had come down, would they have
believed? Yes, I think they would. What
an amazing miracle! Here was a man nailed
to the cross, coming down to the ground.
Who, indeed, could stop to argue about it?
Whose imagination would not be stunned
by it? Whose reason would not be suborned?
Who would be able to ask himself, "Is this
the kind of moral miracle that you expect
of God?" Who, in the presence of such a
miracle, would not have been silenced? *For
an hour or two.* And then? Then they
would have found themselves doubtful. They
would have said, "There was some mistake.
We were drunk; we were mad. It did not
really happen. He was not really nailed to
the cross at all. There was some jugglery.
The executioners were bribed." And belief
would have died. Would the world have
believed? There would have been some
story perhaps, of an obscure execution in
Palestine, of some man who by jugglery or
bribery was able to escape death. Do you
think you would have believed that this took
place, two thousand years ago, or been moved
by it if you did believe? It was by dying
on the cross that Christ moved the world,
because then he appealed to love and with
love, as love alone can appeal. Had he

descended from the cross, that miracle would have undone all his work. The world would never have been moved by a conjurer. It was because he stayed there that the world has been moved to its very heart by Jesus Christ.

Do you see the difference? The one method would have been a spectacular attack on the intelligence, an attempt to force a judgment, to make us believe. It is as though you should knock a man down and stun him and then appeal to his intellect! If such a miracle had taken place it would have stunned the reason. But the appeal that Christ made was something which could only be prejudiced by such a miracle. The world would have passed by, and rightly, saying, "This has nothing to do with us. It is a trick." But by staying there, hanging on the cross, Christ made that eternal appeal to which the heart responds as it knows how. The thief on the one hand sees the Son of God, and the other thief sees only a more contemptible convict than himself. One soldier cries out, "Verily this was the Son of God," and another, sitting at the foot of the cross, plays dice for his clothes. Half the world sees in this Christ a visionary and a dreamer, and the other half sees in him God. But the appeal to all is the same and must eternally be the same. It is to a moral issue and to your power of judging a moral issue. It is no attempt on the part of God to take your personality and force you, stun you, into acquiescence. It is an appeal to your free judgment, and you respond to it as you choose.

When we have crucified God, we say, " Come down from the cross. Do something astonishing. Force us to believe in you if you want us to believe." Do you not see this is what love can never do ? It is not love if it does. So God himself was on the cross when Jesus Christ was crucified two thousand years ago and now is. He is " the Lamb slain from the foundations of the world." He is crucified when one man is shot a few hundred yards from here, or when a negro boy is lynched in Georgia. Wherever human beings suffer, they suffer their own little suffering—hard enough, God knows, to bear. But he is crucified for and in all, and we ask, " Why does he not come down and *make* us act more reasonably and nobly ? Why does he not force us to believe in him ? " Why ? Do you not know that that moral freedom of yours to choose or reject God is the noblest thing about you ? The animals it has been said, dream of moral responsibility ; the plants, a little lower on the slopes

100

of life, are still asleep, safe from suffering and from freedom. But we are called to the high ascent, to higher acts of moral freedom. Is it for us to say to God, " This gift that you gave us we do not desire " ? That is the plea of the slave within us ! It is the everlasting coward that shrinks from freedom.

We indeed cannot understand the awful patience of God, but that is because we do not love enough, not because he loves too little. There are people who cannot understand the love of a mother which survives every kind of cruelty and ingratitude. It is to them incomprehensible. They say she ought to cast her son off. But she does not —not because she does not love him, but because she does. I sometimes think that a son who is won back by his parents' love and sees in their ravaged faces what his redemption has cost them who brought him into the world and gave him his freedom, must understand a little of what the love of God costs him, who does not destroy us when we starve Russia, who does not destroy us because he loves us with a love that we cannot begin to understand.

We get a glimpse of it in the love of our friends who help us merely by loving us. Thus do they show us the love of God. Have

you ever loved anyone ? Well, then, what
did your love do for them ? Has anyone ever
loved you ? What has their love done for
you ? It is not that they have made you
do this, or that, or the other. It is—what
is it ? How can one put into words what
love does for a human being ? Will you
not say to your friend, " It is not what you
do for me. It is not what you give to me.
It is just that you do love me." That is all.
One cannot get any further, but we know
that such a love is everything and all the
world to us, quite apart from anything our
friends do. For love itself does everything.

So is it with the love of God. That he
does not force you does not mean that he
does nothing for you. The fact that he
loves you, like the fact that your friend
loves you, does everything. Why, if your
friend could not do anything to help but
love you, would not you say to him, " The
fact that you love me is everything ? " What
else God does we cannot know or measure,
but the fact that he loves us implies and
involves all the rest.

Here is the world. Look at it. Russia is
starving, and people say : " Why does not
God give food to Russia ? " In the *Manchester
Guardian* I remember reading a report of
a Russian woman who said, on hearing that

America was heaped high with corn, " What kind of a god is it that gives corn in America and lets us starve in Russia ? " Well, when people are starving they say anything. But English people know that there are millions of bushels of corn on one side of the world and ships lined up for lack of work, while there are starving people in Russia. Then they say to one another, " Why does not *God* feed Russia ? " Why do not *we* feed Russia ? Is God to force us by some moral conjuring trick to love and care when we do not love or care ? Is he to make us puppets ? This is what we are continually asking, with our strange and horrible fear of freedom. I call it horrible, for surely it is a betrayal of the best in us to ask that God should *force* us to do this and that.

" Let him teach us," some of you say, " to understand him." I tell you that his meaning and his purpose are written right over the universe. They blaze in the stars, they sound in the waves of the sea. He has written so that only the blind cannot see. " If that is so," you say, " then we are blind. God should make us see." *We* make this world into disorder and say, " Now we cannot see God." *We* shut our eyes, and then we say we cannot see God.

If you misuse your powers you lose them,

If you will not see God, if you do not care
to see him, if you let your mind be guided
by anything except God, you do lose the
power of seeing him, and it would be moral
coercion to "make you see" him. You
know, I suppose, that almost everyone is
born with a fairly correct ear for music,
yet if some of you were to go to learn to sing
and you sang out of tune, you would say,
"I have no ear." But your singing master
very likely would say to you, "You cannot
sing in tune in the middle register of your
voice because you have always sung and
sung badly in the middle register. All the
popular songs and choruses and hymns are
written for the middle notes. You ruin the
middle notes of your voice, so that you
cannot any longer sing these notes properly ;
but the notes you did not use—the high and
low notes—you can use quite well because
you have not spoilt them." So it is not your
ear that is at fault, or not at the beginning.
It is simply the way in which you have mis-
used your voice and your ear by careless
singing. We misuse our power of seeing
moral issues also. We confuse our moral
judgment. We are indifferent to our spiritual
sight, and then our sight gets blurred and
we cannot see God. Then comes the time
when we say, " If God wants me to under-

stand him, why doesn't He *make* me understand him ? If he is speaking to me, why doesn't he force me to hear him ? " He gave you eyes to see him, ears to hear, a spiritual sense to discern him with ; but he will never invade the will and *force* you to hear. He will not coerce your judgment and *make* you understand.

> " Sure he that made us with such large discourse,
> Looking before and after gave us not
> This capability and godlike reason
> To fust in us unused."

I believe that everyone who has heard the voice of God will agree with me in saying that they have a sense that they had been hearing it all the time. If you try to find God and you find him, you will suddenly realise that he was there all the time, and not only that he was there, but that you knew he was. If you were travelling to the sea and suddenly you heard the sound of the sea, you would realise that it had been sounding a long time, and that in some unconscious depths of your being you had heard it. When it breaks in upon your understanding, you know you heard it long ago. So when you suddenly see God, or for a moment hear his voice, it comes with a sense that you had heard it before, but it was in the unconscious depths of your being, and you were so busy with other things, so distracted with other thoughts, that that sounding voice was shut out from your consciousness. It was there all the time. Yes, and you heard it all the time. But it is only when you give yourself to hearing it that you know you hear it. It is that last act—not that God does not speak to you, not that you do not hear, but that you *realise* you hear—it is that last act of giving which *you* must do. God himself cannot do it unless he is to destroy your moral judgment altogether. He never ceases to speak to you ; you never cease to have ears to hear, nerves to carry the message, a brain to understand ; but you can, if you like, shut out that sound. You may become oblivious to the crash of the waves of the sea. And that last act of the will, which is the realisation of that eternal sound, that is for you to make, and God himself cannot *force* you to hear without destroying your moral freedom.

Anything less than the eternal patience of God, and your moral judgment would cease to exist. Your personality would be stunned by the greatness of God. Does not it ever strike you what infinite fineness there must be in the love of God that he does wait for you to " come to yourself " ? What eternal,

what amazing love, that God can look upon
this world and see the use that we have made
of our freedom and the way we torture each
other and ourselves. Every blow we strike
at our brother is a blow at the heart of God,
and yet he leaves us free, yet he waits and
suffers and we cry out that this eternal
patience is the proof of his indifference.
" Come down," we say, " from the cross that
we may see and believe."

I suppose it is really because we cannot
understand a love that *never* varies that the
love of God seems to us non-existent. But
those who love surely must be able to explain
to the world how love uses its power, how it
gives us all we have that is worth having,
how all human joy and all human nobility
depends on the freedom which love allows.
We shall understand at last that it is the
slave in us which cries out to eternal Love
to force us to understand, to compel us to
listen. " Come down from the cross that
we may see and believe."

WHAT IS A CHRISTIAN?

I HAVE given out a good many notices to-night, but I do not grudge the time so much as I might otherwise, since they almost provide me with a text. People sometimes wonder that a church or a religious fellowship should be the centre of so many activities, but if there is one thing that seems to me to stand out from the pages of the New Testament it is that you cannot be a Christian alone. Christianity is a social religion, and I think the loveliest thing that has happened in this Fellowship has been the friendliness that most people tell me they feel when they come into it.

There was an article in one of the religious papers a little while ago on the Guildhouse Services, the writer of which seemed to be thoroughly annoyed with almost everything that happened. He or she did not like the music, did not like the sermon, did not like the preacher's voice and did not like the way the preacher gave out the announcements. But the writer ended, to my surprise, in a way that blotted out all the rest : " There

is a home-like feeling at the Guildhouse."
It is that feeling which is supremely what a
Christian place of worship ought to create,
and if it does that it does not really matter
whether I give out the notices badly, or
whether people do not like Mr. Martin Shaw's
hymns. We have achieved the real spirit
of Christianity if people feel friendly here,
and I have had many letters from people who
say that we have done this. Even people
who have never spoken to anyone here still
feel they are among friends. One letter—I
hope the writer will forgive me for quoting
from it—thanks me for the service here and
goes on to say, " I would like also to thank
the congregation for their part in the happiness
I have received, both at Kensington and the
Guildhouse." Now that sort of thing no
minister can do, no official can do. It rests
entirely with you yourselves, and if you have
made any lonely person feel, as I know
scores of them do feel, that they come here
as to a home every Sunday evening, you are
already nine-tenths of the way to understanding the answer to the question I have
put to-night, " What is a Christian ? "

If you take one of the greatest chapters
in the Bible, you will find that the answer
to that question is, in much lovelier language,
just what I have been trying to say.

" Beloved, let us love one another : for love is of God ; and everyone that loveth is born of God, and knoweth God. He that loveth not knoweth not God ; for God is love. . . ."

" Beloved, if God so loved us, we ought also to love one another. No man hath seen God at any time. If we love one another God dwelleth in us and His love is perfected in us."*

Therefore, if you come to the Guildhouse and do not see God—if neither in the music, nor the sermon, nor the prayers is there any message or vision of God for you, yet if you have felt friendly to other people, God dwelleth in you, for God is love. " No man hath seen God at any time. If we love one another, God dwelleth in us ; for God is love."

Christ revealed God to us just as a human being could. At least I believe that he worked under the ordinary limitations that human beings have to work under. He did not know everything. He did not know what modern science has taught us. About the ordinary facts of the formation of the world and the nature of the stars, and theories of evolution, and so on, our Lord did not know more than any other man of his time and

* 1 John iv, 6, 7, 8, 11, 12.

age knew. He was asked once when the end of the world should come, when he should return to glory. He said he did not know. He worked under human limitations of power and strength. He had to deal with individuals. He healed people who were able to be healed. He was sometimes tired. Not often. He evidently had magnificent health. But he *was* sometimes weary; he had to rest; he had to sleep. He needed to eat and drink. He could only be in one place at a time. He could not see *all* the people who wanted to see him. They often pressed upon him; he had not time to see them all. He worked just like any human being who should be filled with the divine spirit. Of course, he seems to transcend human limitations, but I do not believe that he did. I believe when he told us we ought to be able to do as he did he meant it. He meant that every human being had as much control over circumstances, over his body, over the world in which he lived, as he himself, and that he was showing us what God meant humanity to be like. But his spirit was the spirit of God. " In the beginning was the Word, and the Word was with God, and the Word was God.* Christ shows us what the spirit of God was like. And what was it like ?

*St. John, i, 1.

III

It was a spirit of power and love and joy; of serenity and hope and faith; a spirit of service, a spirit of love for every human being and for every created thing; a spirit of wisdom which understood what was important and what was not important; a spirit divine, joyful, wise, loving, merciful, strong. "That," says Christ, "is what God is like." And when I ask the question, "What is a Christian?" my answer is, "A Christian is a person who is like Christ."

Well, you say, what a platitude! We did not come here on a frightfully hot Sunday evening to listen to such a platitude as that! I wish to God it were a platitude, for every day I find people whose idea of what constitutes a Christian is quite different and absolutely heart-rending. It is heart-rending because it often makes them feel that they themselves can never hope to be Christians : more heart-rending because it often makes them feel that they have no desire to be Christians. Someone told me the other day that a friend of hers was going into an office—where, I do not know or how it happened to be what she described—but she said with some alarm that that place was a "perfect den of Christians," by which I gathered that she meant it was a place of profound gloom, of people who make mountains out of molehills, who thought that God cares about such futile, ridiculous trifles as none but a very foolish and tiresome human being could make a fuss about. " A den of Christians ! " Is it really a platitude to say that a Christian is a person who is like Christ ?

A member of the congregation once described to me her mother. She said, " She is the kind of woman to whom everyone takes their difficulties." Not a rich woman, not perhaps, a highly educated woman, but a woman to whom you instinctively went, knowing that she would never leave you in a hole. And after having described to me this mother, she said sorrowfully, " But she isn't at all religious." Good God ! What is religion if that is not religion ? What do you mean by a Christian if that is not a Christian ? I said to her, " What can you mean by saying that a woman whose whole life is full of service to God and man is not religious ? " And after some thought, she said, " Well, she never goes to church." I do not think our Lord said very much about going to church. He went himself, I suppose, until they drove him out. And I am certain that every Christian desires to find fellowship with other Christians and sometimes to meet them and worship God together. But that is because we *want* to do it, because we like

113

to do it. To do it because it is a duty seems to me to be a most extraordinary idea of God. As though one would go to see one's friend from a sense of duty! One goes because one *wants* to go, and in any case our Lord said very little about it. But he continually taught us in every parable, in every saying, and in the whole of his own life that religion consisted in serving our fellow-men. In that great parable of the sheep and the goats, you remember, the ones who were welcome in Heaven were the ones who had served their fellow-men, and the ones who were cast out were the ones who had not served. There is nothing whatever about going to church, or about believing any special doctrine, unless you call believing in love a doctrine. It is, of course, the greatest of all beliefs. But that is the only one on which our Lord laid very much stress.

On the other hand, some years ago I heard a man discussed who had just resigned his bishopric, and two clergy of his diocese were nearly frantic with joy because he was going. They kept interrupting themselves, because they were really very kind, good men, and saying, " It is a shame to talk like this, because he really is such a Christian." I said, " In what sense is he a Christian ? " " Well," they said, " of course he is dreadfully narrow-

minded and domineering." I said, " But
surely Christ wasn't narrow-minded and domineering ? " " Well," they said, " no, that is
true. But, you know, he does say so many
prayers." Afterwards they added thought-
fully, " It is generally when he has said the
most prayers that he does something out-
rageous." I said, " I should like to know
what he is praying, what his God is like, and
in what way this person resembles Christ,
who is narrow-minded and domineering."
I sometimes think our Lord's hatred of
making a fuss about trifles was one of the
strongest things in his character. Yon
remember that when the Pharisees objected
because his disciples plucked ears of wheat
on a sabbath day, they said it was against
the ecclesiastical law, and I feel that almost
anyone else would have said to his disciples,
" Don't pluck ears of wheat on the sabbath.
You are offending very sincere, religious
people, and after all you cannot really mind
whether you pluck ears of corn or not, so just
don't." But he would not. He said to
the Pharisees in so many words, " Do not
make a fuss about trifles. That is not what
God cares about. That is not religion. The
sabbath was made for man, not man for the
sabbath." Almost always people to-day, when
they find great importance attached to some

trifle, say, " Well, it is only a trifle after all.
It is better to yield on these points." I
wonder if it is ? I sometimes think that the
really important issue is that nobody should
be allowed to think that God cares about
such little things, about such trifles as whether
a person plucks ears of wheat on a Saturday
or a Sunday. It is the disfiguring of God
in our minds that made Christ so angry, that
made him refuse to yield to what we should
say was such a little point. After all, he
came to reveal God to us, and to be a Christian
is to be able to reveal God also to other
people. It does not really matter about the
rites and ceremonies of religion. I do not
say they have no importance. I think they
have : they have a psychological importance :
they have an importance also from a religious
point of view. But they are not the first
things.

I think of another friend of mine who became
a Christian in very difficult circumstances.
Her family practically cut her off, cast her
out. She had not much health. She had
not much education. But they turned her
out and left her to earn her living in a poor
state of health, without any training. She
really did sacrifice about as much for Christ
as most people do ! Yet another woman
told her she was not really a Christian at all,

because she had only been baptised by having a little water poured upon her instead of by total immersion ! Is that not un-Christlike ? Some people would rule out the whole of the Society of Friends, which has in it some of the best Christians in the world, because they have never been baptised at all. They have only loved God and served their fellow men. They have only done those things which our Lord did all his life, and which he told us were religion.

People come to me who want to join some Christian Church, perhaps they want to join the Church of England, and they take up the Confirmation Service and find they have to believe in the Virgin Birth, and they do not. They do believe in Christ, and they are Christlike. And we have to wonder whether they can stretch their belief enough to fit the creed, instead of stretching their lives enough to fit Christ ! Christ only asked of his disciples that they should love him, and to love him is to be like him, because you cannot love a person with whom you have nothing at all in common. If you love anyone, you have something of their spirit. It is true that our Lord loved clear thinking as well. When St. Peter answered that he knew who Jesus was, one can see from the joy with which our Lord hailed his words that he does care that we should care about the truth. But he did not turn to the other disciples and say, "*You* have not found this out, so you must go away. You have not got the right Christology. You have not given the right answer." He said, that St. Peter had had it revealed to him by the Holy Spirit of God and that gave him joy. But all the disciples loved him, and all of them had a little of his spirit, and that was what he asked of people who were going to follow him.

Do not these other things matter? Yes, of course, they matter. It matters tremendously what you think of Christ. But let us put first things first. To be a Christian is to be like Christ. You may never have heard of Christ. The great catholic poet of the Middle Ages, Dante, looking for the best in mankind, could not refrain from taking four or five of the great noble pagans who had never heard the name of Jesus Christ and putting them into his purgatory or his paradise because they were souls naturally Christlike. And all over the world there are lovers of Christ who have the spirit of God in them, and have never heard of Jesus of Nazareth. Yes, and there are people here who reject him. I will tell you why they reject him in what is called Christian England.

They reject Christ because Christians—so-called Christians—have so misrepresented him. It is as true of them that they have never seen Christ as it was of Plato, or Confucius, or Buddha. It is almost worse, because they have seen Christians—so-called Christians—who are such a caricature of Christ, whose whole idea of religion is bound up with little rules and ceremonies, and who are cruel, and hard, and intolerant to others. It seems to me that these two sets of Christians, the Christians who have never heard of Christ and the Christians who have seen Christ caricatured, and therefore reject him, come under these great sayings of our Lord :

" Other sheep I have, which are not of this fold : them also I must bring . . . and there shall be one fold and one shepherd."*

Or again,

" Whosoever shall speak a word against the Son of Man, it shall be forgiven him : but unto him that blasphemeth against the Holy Spirit, it shall not be forgiven."†

* St. John x, 16.   † St. Luke xii, 10.

SOME FORMS OF WORSHIP

" Thou shalt love the Lord Thy God with all thy heart and with all thy soul and with all thy mind and with all thy strength."

I AM going to preach to-night about forms of worship and especially about the forms we use here in the Guildhouse ; and for my text I take the above words.

Worship is the soul's response to God. It is nothing formal, nothing, in a sense, to do with creeds, nothing doctrinal, nothing forced. It is not, in a sense, a "duty." It is the spontaneous emotion of love and praise and wonder that goes out to things that are worshipful, wonderful and lovely. "We live by admiration, hope and love." That is worship, and every form of worship, every religious service, ought so to express God that irresistibly the minds of those who are present are moved to love and worship. That is the supreme aim of a religious service, that you should so see God, even if only for a moment of silence or a moment of praise, that you ask nothing more. You no longer want to get anything out of him, you do not seek to change his mind ; your heart simply goes out in a passion of love and joy. To create that feeling should be the aim of every religious service.

Perhaps some of you wonder why, in that case, we need to have a service at all. It is easier for some people to worship God when they look at a rainbow ; to worship him on the top of a mountain ; to feel their hearts go out in love and awe when they see the starlit skies at night, or the great spaces of the sea. And it may be much more difficult to let your heart go out like that to God among other human beings, whom perhaps you do not like very much ; who are not half as beautiful as the starlit sky or the sea ; who cough and sneeze and push and get on your nerves. Canon Scott Holland once said, " As for loving our brother whom we have seen, it is just because we have seen him that we find it so difficult ! " I suppose everyone, in every place of worship, finds something that jars, or at least it is quite possible that he may do so. However the service is arranged, something or somebody will jar and you will wish you had sought God where you could worship him undisturbed, where there would be nothing between your soul and his presence, where you could, in praise and worship, let your soul go out in mystical communion. Certainly we ought to do that too. " The heavens declare the glory of God, and the firmament showeth his handiwork," and everyone should sometimes worship God in natural beauty. We ought not to build our cities so big that people cannot get out of them to see God, or the houses so high and our streets so narrow that we cannot see the sky. Everyone ought to worship God on the top of a mountain. But see him also in human beings ! God is not only in illimitable space ; he is in you, he is in me ; he is in our friends, our mothers, our children, our teachers. God is in human faces. You ought not to be able to look at a human being and not see God. That is where he really speaks to you. You can see him in Nature, yes, that is easy ; but can you not see him also in the human heart ? It was one of the greatest of all mystics who wrote of the human quality of love. No one saw God in the mountain tops more than Blake did, who wrote that wonderful little hymn, one of the loveliest we ever sing here :—

Mercy, Pity, Peace, and Love,
Is God our Father dear.
And Mercy, Pity, Peace, and Love
Is man, His child and care.

For Mercy has a human heart,
  Pity a human face.
And Love the human form divine,
  And Peace a human dress.

Thus every man of every clime,
  That prays in his distress,
Prays to the human form divine,
  Love, Mercy, Pity, Peace.

And all must love the human form,
  In heathen, Turk or Jew,
Where Mercy, Love and Pity dwell,
  There God is dwelling too.

Is not that true of everyone? Did not God speak to some of you first through your mother's eyes? Or did not the first time come to others through a lover or a friend? When Samuel heard the voice of God he thought it was the voice of his best friend. Has that ever struck you? He said to his old friend Eli, " You called me." But it was God who had called him, though it sounded like the voice of his friend. Do you know that touching little Irish story about a woman who was in great distress of mind because she had lost the sense of God? She said, " Why doesn't he make me feel that he is there? How can he leave me alone? If I could only feel him, know that he had touched me!" And an old woman who was sitting with her said, " Pray to him. Ask him to touch you. He will put his hand on

123

you." She began to pray in agony, and suddenly felt the hand of God touching her. She cried out, " He has touched me ! " and went into an ecstasy of joy. Then she said, " But do you know, it felt just like your hand ? " And the old woman said, " Why, it was my hand." " It was your hand ? " " Sure, what did you think God would be doing ? Did you think he would make a long arm out of heaven to touch you ? *He just took the hand that was nearest and used that.*" Is that not the beginning of the religious life of millions of people ? God takes the human beings that are nearest, and through them for the first time we see love, and love is God. He takes the human hand of some friend or stranger and uses that, and for the first time we feel the touch of God. We say, " It is only a friend ! " What do we mean by God if it is not Love ? How can God speak to us but by a human voice ?

When you come together to worship God with other human beings, do you not get the sense of God—you should—from the fact that others of his children are there with you in the same building ? There is a power where there are a number of people together finding God, which is absent when one is alone. That is not an arbitrary rule of ecclesiastics, to get you to come to church.

When our Lord said, " Where two or three are gathered together, there am I in the midst of them," he said something that every psychologist to-day knows to be true. The sense that is in us here to-night is something more than the sense that each of us would have alone. We are drawn together here into one place ; it is God who is drawing us, and when we come together we find him in a different way, not a better or worse way perhaps, but just a different way from that in which we find him when we are alone. And we cannot ever find enough of God. There is not one of us that will ever get so far that he understands the whole of God. God is too great, too mighty for us. But that means that we must seek him in every way. Do not forget to seek him in solitude, but do not forget either to seek him with your friends, even with strangers, because they too are human beings, and because human beings are the children of God they will help you to find him, and to get that common sense of God which should make every person who goes out of this hall more sure of God than when he came in.

So we ought to have a great deal of praise in a public service. The love and joy that arise when you see God should be expressed in praise. There ought to be singing. At any rate there ought to be some way of expressing joy, because we ought to think more of God than ourselves, more even than of our own unworthiness. I do not think that we ought to begin a public service of worship by confessing our sins. I do not think that is the way that penitence really arises in the human soul. I always feel the right place for a confession of sin is that in which it comes in the Holy Communion Service of the Church of England ; not at the beginning, but just before the climax, for it is when we are closest to God that we are most sorry for what we have done wrong. When we compare ourselves with one another we shall always find someone a little worse than ourselves ; but when we come near to God, that cry of St. Peter's, " Depart from me for I am a sinful man ! " breaks from our lips. And so at the Holy Communion Service, when we are just approaching the altar, then is the moment when penitence breaks over us like a flood.

But if a service should begin with praise, it is clear that we need forms. If we are going to sing, we simply must sing the same thing ! We cannot all sing the tune that comes into our heads—I know some people do, but it does not have a really good effect. It is better all to sing the same tune and words. Consequently, we must have our praises written down. Then we have forms of prayers, too, and I want to explain why. It is really a question of fellowship. We cannot so easily pray together when we do not know what the prayer is going to say. When I pray after this sermon, *ex tempore*, as it is called, there has to be a certain effort of attention to follow what I am saying and to join your mind with mine. But when you know the prayer, you can pray all the time. " Our Father, who art in heaven "—you can *think* it all as you go along. And so, although at first sight it seems to some people very formal and artificial, a written form of prayer is really a fundamental element in the social life of the Church. It enables us to pray together. Did you ever consider that the great old prayers of the Christian Church have been the way by which souls have come home to God for hundreds and hundreds of years? When you say, " Our Father, which art in heaven," you are coming to God by the path that was trodden by St. John, by St. Francis, by St. Theresa, by St. Catherine, by Saint Joan of Arc, by all the saints. When you take on your lips the words of the Psalms, or the words of some ancient canticle or prayer, you are experiencing the communion of the saints, for by the same path that their

spirits trod, your soul seeks God. The words
that expressed their need meet your need
also. You are bound to them and to all
those unnumbered unknown saints, humble
people, whose names you do not know, but
in whose spiritual communion you take part
when you join in the prayers of the Church.
It is a bond of fellowship to use a common
prayer.

Then there ought also to be what is called
ex tempore prayer ; because the greatest *old*
prayer in the world cannot bring before God
just what happened last week, or what is
going to happen next week, and God's love
cares for us individually and for our individual
needs as well as for the great common needs
of all humanity. He cares about the people
who are out of work to-day, and the people
who are ill and lonely ; and about the
Washington Conference, and the Irish Conference, and all the things that are happening
to-day. So that, in order to deepen our
sense of God and our communion with one
another, we want to pray about the things
that are happening now. And when I pray
here *ex tempore* I try to think of all the things
that have been weighing on your hearts and
mine during the past week, and will weigh
on our hearts during the coming week, and
to bring them to God, knowing that these

cares, some great, some small, are to him as urgent and as dear as the great human needs that are expressed by the great traditional prayers of the Church.

Then there ought also to be a silence in our worship. There are people here of every kind of opinion. People who have no personal God and people to whom God is supremely personal ; and people who have come to find out whether there be any God at all. But all of us can unite in that moment of silence. All of us are looking for the truth, whether we call it God or not, and any words that we can use are clumsy to express Truth ; any word will sometimes seem wrong and will therefore divide us. But in the silence there is nothing to divide. All over the world there are people like you and me, hungering for God, finding him in one Church or another, in one religion or another, or outside any religion but still thirsting for God. And in that moment of silence at the end of the prayers, we seek to unite our souls with all those who are seeking for the truth, and to pray with them and for them that we may never desire anything that is not true, but at whatever cost may seek truth and ensue it.

That is briefly the underlying idea of our Guildhouse service, but there is something more ; there is the effort to create such a service as will give us both fellowship and devotion ; that will, in a word, give us the love of our fellow men, friendliness, familiarity and fellowship, and at the same time the sense of the transcendent God who is above and greater than the God in our hearts. It is exceedingly difficult ; I want to admit that. Most of you have found it so already. It is difficult to create an atmosphere in which are equally present the sense of fellowship with one another, and the sense of the presence and communion of God. Because—at least I think this is why—religion has so long been associated with gloom and fear. Some psychologists tell us that all religion was born of fear ; the savage man's fear of the dark ; the fear of the unknown ; the fear of death : that religion took its rise not out of the hunger of the heart for God, but out of the fear of the unknown. I am not going to discuss it at the moment, though I do not believe it. But it has this element of truth, that in most religions there is a strong element of fear, and consequently to most people a service that is cheerful easily seems a service that is irreverent. They are accustomed to a certain solemnity — my mind reverting to some churches I have been in, I might almost say a gloom ! And we find a difficulty in being perfectly at home in the presence of God,

and yet having an intense sense of his greatness, beauty and wonder. And it is the
supreme aim of all those who care about
this Guildhouse to find the way by which we
can be equally in communion with God and
man. I repeat, it is difficult. To begin with,
we must have nothing that breaks our sense
of fellowship ; we must have all that promotes
it. Other churches have other ways, but
personally I do not like pew rents and sittings
allotted to certain people, just because it is
so apt to make the people who have not paid
a pew rent and have not an allotted seat,
feel outside. For that reason I do not like
it. I want everyone to feel that every seat
is the right seat to sit in, and I do not want
anyone else to look at them in amazement
when they sit down, as much as to say, " I
have paid for that seat and you do not belong
there." It is not necessary to do that if you
have a pew, I know, but it is unfortunately
common. It is really terrifying to go into
some churches, because of the fear of sitting
on the wrong seat ! That is why we do not
have pew rents here. We do not want to
break the sense of fellowship.

We like to talk while the collection is being
taken. People say, " Wouldn't it be better
to be silent during the collection ? When we
took money for the Russian famine we took

it in silence, and what a wonderful effect it had!" We took that collection in silence because we were giving an infinitesimal gift to a ghastly human need, the greatest need the world has ever seen. It was surely fitting to take it in silence. But when we take a collection for the Guildhouse, is there anything so very depressing about that? "No," you say, "but it is a gift to God." Can you not give to God without being solemn? Give to God joyfully and cheerfully, and at the same time give to your neighbour an expression of friendship in conversation. What is the kingdom of God but happiness and friendship and joy?

Can we not get fellowship with one another without losing the sense of God? Is it impossible? It is for you to answer. To me it seems not impossible. If I have ever lost the sense of God in this building I have always known it was my own fault. I cannot believe it is because people are talking around me. After all, they are looking for God too, in their different ways. I believe it is possible to have such a service as would be full of joy and ease and the sense of being at home —because it is God's house, it is our house too, since we are his children—and yet to have here more intensely than in any other place the sense of the transcendent God. It is difficult because all our traditions are the other way. The idea of solemnity in connection with religion is so deeply ingrained. We can hardly believe that Jesus ever laughed, and yet how often he must have laughed ! What indescribable gaiety of heart there must have been in that little band as they went about the country preaching the Kingdom of God ! So I will not believe it is impossible for us to be full of gaiety here, and yet full of God. It is what we are dreaming of for the Guildhouse, and will you who come help us to achieve it ? I am told sometimes that we had a greater sense of God when we worshipped in that ugly, inconvenient Town Hall in Kensington than we have here. I do not know, but if it is true it proves how entirely the creation of that sense of God lies with us, and how little it really matters where we are. If we were conscious of God, no one would come into this Guildhouse without being conscious of him too. We know God is everywhere, but we forget. We want to come where we shall remember, and if we remember that he is here no one who comes into this place will be able to forget. Fellowship demands that we shall sometimes talk to each other, but it also demands that we should sometimes be silent ; that we should not disturb those who desire to pray ; that we should not be talking in the wrong place and so make it difficult for other people to be at peace. If there were a real silence before our worship begins, silence in the middle, and silence during the prayers, this should make it easy for people to realise the presence of God.

I cherish this hope for the Guildhouse and I think it is partly true already, that no one who comes here will feel an outsider, unfamiliar, strange, unwanted. I trust that everyone who comes in will be made to feel by all the rest, not in words, but by that indescribable atmosphere of friendliness, that they are at home; so that when we go out from here men will know that we and they have been with Jesus.

THE SPIRIT OF CHRISTMAS

" Now abideth faith, hope, love . . . and the greatest of these is love."—1 Cor. xiii, 13.

I AM sorry to have to destroy the beautiful cadence of the English Authorised Version, " Now abideth faith, hope, charity ; but the greatest of these is charity " ; but I do not think that the word " charity " is really redeemable ; we have made it so chilly that I cannot bring myself, much as I love the Authorised Version, to use it in this passage. " Now abideth faith, hope, love ; but the greatest of these is love."

I wanted to read you a story this afternoon, but I cannot find it anywhere. It is a Russian story. I think I must have met it probably in Dostoëvsky's novels or short stories. I will try to tell it to you. It is a story very Russian in spirit, a story of a woman who was very respectable and highly respected. She did everything that she ought, and in the fulness of time she died and went to hell. Yes, she was quite as much surprised as you are. In fact she was so overwhelmed with surprise that she made more hubbub at the gates of hell than any other person who has ever been there. She made such a riot that at last the Eternal Father heard her and said to one of the angels, " What is all that noise about ? " The angel replied, " Somebody has gone to hell who thinks she ought not to be there. She says there must be some mistake." " That's not very likely," said the Eternal Father, and he turned his mind to other things. But the noise went on and on until at last he said to the angel, " Just go and see whether there really has been any mistake." So the angel went down, and asked the woman what was the matter. She explained that all her life she had been highly respectable and deeply respected, and there must be some mistake about her destination. The angel returned to the Eternal Father, and told him what the woman had said. " Ask her," he answered, " whether she has ever done anything kind to anybody." The angel flew down again and said to the old woman, " Did you ever do anything kind to anybody ? " Then she had to think a long time. She began again to say that she was highly respectable and deeply respected. " But," he said, " have you done anything kind ? " After a long time her face brightened, and she said, " Yes : I once gave an onion to a tramp." The angel returned to

136

the Eternal Father. "She says she once gave an onion to a tramp." "An onion is always something," said the Eternal Father. "Take that onion and go down to her and hold it out, and tell her if she holds on you will draw her up to heaven." The angel took the onion and went down, and said to the woman, "Here is your onion. Hold on and I will draw you up to heaven." The woman held on, you can imagine! And the angel began to draw her up to heaven. But when the other people in hell saw that, they ran to the old woman and held on to her skirts and others came and held on to each other, and as the angel began to soar up into heaven, all the inhabitants of hell rose up after him. When the old woman saw that, she was frightened. "Let go!" she said. "Let go! it's my onion!" Alas! when she said "It's my onion," the onion broke, and they all fell back into hell! And now it does not matter how much noise she makes: the Eternal Father doesn't take a bit of notice.

Now, you say, is that a Christmas story? Well, don't you think it is? It is a story for this Christmas, surely! Some of the best of us feel that we can hardly do more, or that we have hardly done as much, as to give an onion to a tramp, and I think that story is singularly like one that might have come out

of one of the four Gospels, with its conviction that the only thing the Eternal Father
really cares about in the last resort is whether
we ever do anything kind to anybody, and
that however highly respectable and deeply
respected you may be, however long your
string of duties done, the thing that really
interests him is the question whether you
ever did anything kind.

It is the story of the sheep and the goats
over again, isn't it ? The goats were the
people who had obviously done their duty as
they saw it, and who were as much surprised
as this old lady to find themselves on the
wrong side ; expressed themselves in just the
same words of indignation. " *When* saw we
thee hungry ? When saw we thee thirsty ?
When saw we thee in prison and afflicted and
visited thee not ? " The final decision is
that those who were kind to one another are
on the right side, and those who were not
kind on the wrong. And at the heart of
parable after parable, and act after act, and
word after word in the Gospels there is this
constant emphasis on the quality of human
kindness. It scandalises many otherwise good
Christians. "Now abideth faith, hope, love;
and the greatest of these is *faith*," nearly all
the theologians have been inclined to say.
So Christians have burned each other in the

name of love, because their faith was not quite correct.

In every nation and in every class there is some special virtue that people pride themselves on, but it is not always kindness. Rich people pride themselves on being clean and having baths frequently, and sometimes on having a high sense of honour. People's sense of honour is often rather arbitrary. The idea that you must not tell a mean kind of lie, and that it is better not to tell some lies at all—this is the standard of the wealthier class. Some people think that personal courage is everything; many men have thought so about men. Others think that chastity is everything; many people have thought so about women. And when our Lord went to talk and sit and eat with harlots and publicans and sinners, people were just as much scandalised as they would be to-day if they saw him do it, just as they are scandalised when they see other people do it. Many of us are like the old country squire in one of Butler's books, of whom the author said that he would have been equally shocked to hear Christianity questioned or to see it practised! Our Lord was often with the rakes and rascals and disreputables; still more often with the poor; and I think it was because he really liked them, not necessarily because he thought

he could do them more good than other
people, but because he really *liked* them, and
I believe almost anyone who has lived with
the very poor will agree with me when I say
that their chief virtue, the one they admire
and practise most, is kindness. They do not
call it love; that sounds rather too big a
word to them perhaps; they call it being
kind, and the highest praise that the poor
ever give to anyone is that he is kind. And
their own chief virtue surely is that they are
kind. I remember when that terrible ex-
plosion took place during the war in Silvertown. The people at Toynbee Hall, which
had at that time a branch in Poplar—nearer
to Silvertown than Whitechapel—were given
the duty of housing those who were left
without homes, and Mr. Heath, then Warden
of Toynbee Hall, told me many women came
whose children had only two changes of
clothes, and gave one of them, because they
did not feel they could possibly keep two sets
of clothing when some children had none at
all. That sort of kindness makes one understand why our Lord loved the poor so much,
and I think also that he loved children
partly because children are kind. Children
sometimes want to hurt, and they often hurt
when they do not mean to; but if you really
appeal to a child's compassion it is extra-

ordinarily kind. Partly also I think Christ loved children because they are the chief incentive to kindness in other people. If our Lord loved kindness so much, it must have given him great joy often to see the Jews, who were so cruel to him, and often so harsh to one another, so mean, so spiteful, so censorious, at their best with their children. There are no homes better than Jewish homes, no parents more truly devoted than Jewish parents. People who were cruel to one another must often have shown our Lord their best side when he saw them with their children. The attitude of Jewish parents to their children has become a proverb in the world for devotion and self-sacrifice, and that makes one realise a little how tremendous has been the meaning to all the world, even to the cruellest and hardest, of the coming of children.

Most of you, I expect, know the story of Silas Marner, who was weaned away from the love of gold by a little child. It sounds sentimental, but it is not. It is so absolutely simple and natural, so inevitable, so much a matter of course, that when somebody is utterly dependent on you, and perfectly guileless and perfectly confident that you are going to do everything for him, then the stoniest-hearted person can hardly remain stony-hearted. That " a little child shall lead them " has been true of individuals, and of all the world. When I was reading just now the story of the shepherds it seemed to me so much the story, really, of the coming of all children into the world. " The angel of the Lord came upon them, and the glory of the Lord shone round about them ; and the angel said unto them, I bring you good tidings of great joy, for unto you is born this day a Saviour, which is Christ the Lord. And this shall be a sign unto you, ye shall find the Babe wrapped in swaddling clothes lying in a manger. And suddenly there was with the angel a multitude of the heavenly host, praising God, and saying, Glory to God in the highest, and in earth peace and goodwill to men." Then the shepherds went in haste, and found Mary and Joseph and the Babe lying in the manger. Such a little homely thing to find, after all the multitude of heaven praising God, and saying " Glory to God in the highest," and yet so absolutely the one thing that does bring peace on earth, goodwill to men. All the stories that centre round our Lord's birth really belong to childhood everywhere. That is why they are immortal, why, whether they are legends or not, they will always remain true in the heart of humanity. The coming of the Wise Men to the cradle of

a child, showing that wisdom, glorious and
godlike as it is, is yet less divine than love :
the coming of the shepherds, to whom the
heavens were opened and the glory of God
made manifest, because a child had been
born : is it not really, in one little episode,
the history of all the world ? Has anything
made us gentle except the necessities of
children ? Has love ever been born except
first of all it was born in the heart of a
mother ? To how many human beings have
the heavens first opened when they knew
there was a child coming ? To how many
nations the hope yet remains of peace on
earth, goodwill amongst men, because there
is still hope, still faith, and still love where
there are children ? Unkindness to them
seemed to our Lord the most abominable of
all sins. Kindness is the one thing, the one
essential thing, that brings you heaven :
unkindness deserves hell, but unkindness to
a child—" it were better that a millstone
had been hung round his neck and he had
been drowned in the depths of the sea."
What a phrase of white anger is that ! Because it is such a peculiarly blasphemous
thing to take that which should lead you to
God, which should be the very incentive of
love, the very fount and inspiration of gentleness in the human race, and treat it with

143

cruelty. It would be better that such a one
were drowned in the sea. "For I say unto
you their angels in heaven do always behold
the face of my Father which is in heaven."
It is not for nothing that these words of white
heat should have come from our Lord about
children, nor is it for nothing that one of
the most moving scenes in history should be
connected with children, and his indignation
when people tried to send them away. Not
to be kind is to be unchildlike, for really, as
I said, children are kind. And for a child to
be hurt, and to have hatred sown in its heart,
is surely the wickedest of all things. To
poison the mind of a grown up person is bad,
but to poison the springs of life in a child's
heart—that is almost unforgivable.

I do not wish to cast any shadow over
this day—to all the world that knows
Christianity at all perhaps the dearest—and
yet I cannot help reflecting that we, un-
consciously I think, are poisoning the minds
of children all over the world by ill-treatment.
I remember the children who starve while
we rejoice to-day. That is why I thought my
story was a good story for this Christmas.
We have done what we could here at the
Guildhouse, but many people to-day are
remembering at their Christmas festivities
the children who are not at any Christmas

144

table, and because they remember them they do not indeed allow it to cloud the festivity (for after all, Christmas is for children and children should be happy), but they have collected a little money at each meal for children in Russia, in Austria, or elsewhere, as a sign of friendliness, a gesture, to hold out a hand of friendship across this great gulf of misery. I had a letter the other day from a friend of mine working in Russia, describing the state of things there, saying what people used to say about Austria in the first days after the war, that even greater than the gift of food was the sense of kindness. Far beyond the material gift, which alas! must be so small in any case, was the preciousness of the sympathy which sent it. Just the human kindliness. It is right, is it not? to think it the greatest of all qualities, for even to starving people, it seems, food is less precious than the kindliness that sends it. The world perishes to-day for lack of a little human kindness. It is full of the cruelty that comes of fear and indignation. Is it not possible on this last Sunday of 1921 that we should a little forget to be so highly respectable and so deeply respected, and instead remember to be a little kind, to bind up the wounds of the world instead of always keeping them open? Let us forget to exact our debts.

145

Let us forgive our debtors. Let us forget at last to execute judgment and let us begin to bind up each other's wounds, and to remember in a common suffering—for after all there is enough suffering in this country also—that there is no quality so redeeming as Love ; to succour each other's children ; to refrain from poisoning the hearts of babes with our international hatreds ; to take the children of the world in our arms, lay our hands on them and bless them.

"Now abideth, faith, hope, love"—all these things we owe to children—our hope for the future, when all the world seems in chaos ; the hope of those who have made a ruin of their lives ; the hope of those for whom the world seems to hold nothing, that at least their children will do better than they did, that at least they can give their children a better chance than they had, that at least the world in which their children will live will be a better world than the world in which they have lived.

And faith : one's faith in human nature is reawakened, confirmed, by being with children. We who are so ignorant, so selfish, so mean, so hard, are shamed into putting a little faith in ourselves and a little faith in other human beings by the exquisite confidence with which a little child will put its hand in ours and let us take it anywhere. Faith in humanity is renewed to those who live with children.

And love : love was born when people sacrificed to bring children into the world, love is sustained when parents sacrifice to give their children a better chance than their own, love is evoked in one's heart by living with children. All these things we owe to children—faith, hope and love, but the greatest of these is love. And to-day and in the coming days let us, I repeat, a little forget the lesser virtues, let us forget to exact justice, and to demand our debts, and let us remember to be kind.